United States
Department of
Agriculture

Forest Service

Southern
Research Station

Resource Bulletin
SRS–156

# North Carolina's Timber Industry— An Assessment of Timber Product Output and Use, 2007

Jason A. Cooper and
Michael C. Mann

I0435018

## The Authors:

**Jason A. Cooper**, Forester, U.S. Forest Service,
Southern Research Station, Knoxville, TN 37919;
**Michael C. Mann**, Utilization Forester, North Carolina
Division of Forest Resources, Raleigh, NC 27699.

July 2009

Southern Research Station
200 W.T. Weaver Blvd.
Asheville, NC 28804

## Foreword

This report contains the findings of a 2007 canvass of all primary wood-using plants in North Carolina, and presents changes in product output and residue use since 2005. It complements the Forest Inventory and Analysis periodic inventory of volume and removals from the State's timberland. The canvass was conducted to determine the amount and source of wood receipts and annual timber product drain, by county, in 2007 and to determine interstate and cross-regional movement of industrial roundwood. Only primary wood-using mills were canvassed. Primary mills are those that process roundwood in log or bolt form or as chipped roundwood. Examples of industrial roundwood products are saw logs, pulpwood, veneer logs, poles, and logs used for composite board products. Mills producing products from residues generated at primary and secondary processors were not canvassed. Trees chipped in the woods were included in the estimate of timber drain only if they were delivered to a primary domestic manufacturer.

A 100-percent canvass of all wood processors in North Carolina was conducted in 2008 to obtain information for 2007. In addition, roundwood from out-of-State mills known to be using logs or bolts harvested from North Carolina timberland was incorporated into North Carolina production estimates. Each mill was canvassed by mail or through personal contact at plant locations. Telephone contacts followed mailed questionnaire responses when additional information or clarification of a response was necessary. In the event of a nonresponse, data collected in previous surveys were updated using current data collected for mills of similar size, product type, and location. Surveys for all timber products other than pulpwood began in 1961, and are currently conducted every 2 years.

Pulpwood production data were taken from an annual canvass of all southern pulpmills. Medium density fiberboard, insulating board, and hardboard plants were included in this survey.

## Acknowledgments

The authors thank Barry New and Don Roach for review and comments; Carolyn Steppleton and Michael Howell for their tireless efforts in processing and accuracy of the data; Helen Beresford for timber product output database maintenance and support; Anne Jenkins, Janet Griffin, Sharon Johnson, and Charlene Walker for tables, graphs, and statistical checking; and the Southern Research Station (SRS) Technical Publications Team for editorial review, styling, and publication of this report.

The SRS gratefully acknowledges the cooperation and assistance provided by the North Carolina Department of Environment and Natural Resources, Division of Forest Resources in collecting mill data. Appreciation is also extended to forest industry and mill managers for providing timber products information.

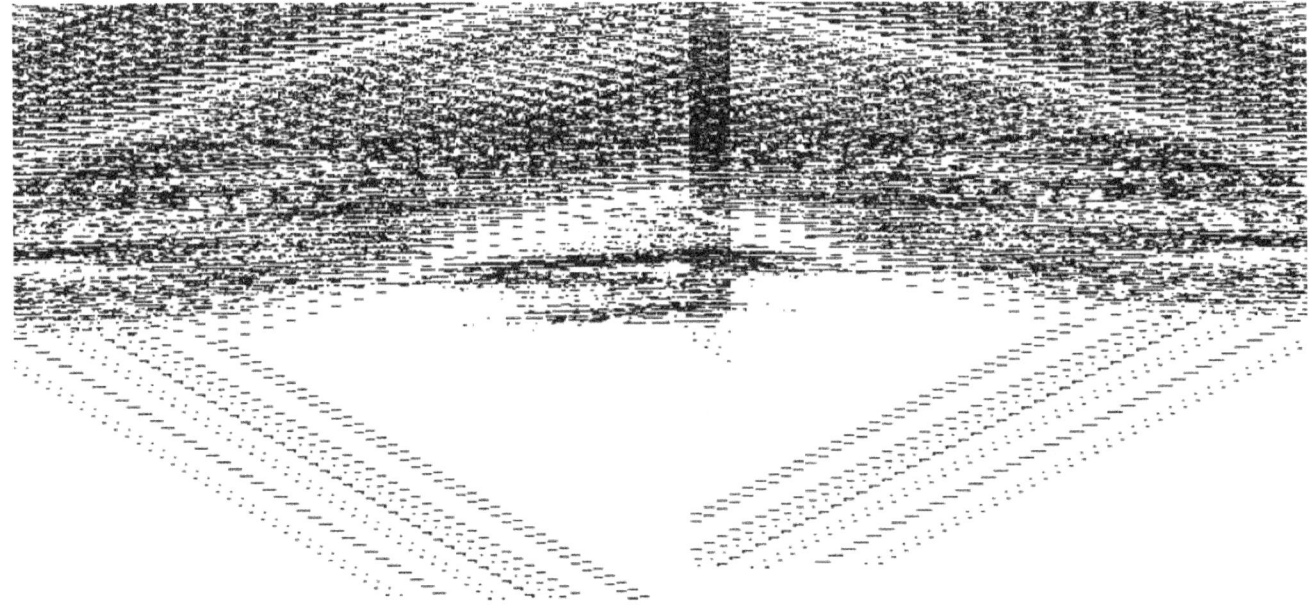

## Timber Product Output Database Retrieval System

The Forest Inventory and Analysis (FIA) Research Work Unit of the USDA Forest Service developed the Timber Product Output (TPO) Database Retrieval System to help customers answer questions about timber harvesting and use in the Southern Region. This system acts as an interface to a standard set of consistently coded TPO data for each State and county in the region and Nation. This regional and national set of TPO data consists of 11 variables that describe for each county the roundwood products harvested, logging residues left in the woods, other timber removals (i.e. land clearing and reserved timber removals), and wood and bark residues generated by the county's primary wood-using mills. The system is available through the FIA Web site: http://srsfia2.fs.fed.us/.

The database is well documented and easy to use. The retrieval system allows the user to select the TPO variables of interest and generate a standard set of timber products, removals, and mill residue tables for the specified resource area, State, or region. The system has been logically divided into two sections to assist the user in making specific data requests. In section 1, the user will be asked to define the resource area, and section 2 generates tables for the specified area. In each section, the user is asked to supply specific options that will serve to customize the database retrieval.

There are four options available for defining the geographic area of interest. Each option provides an increasing level of detail. The region, subregion, State, or county defines an area. The user selects the option that best suits the level of detail required. Users who select county as an option should be aware that some counties have been combined due to data sensitivity. These combined counties are identified with asterisks in the output tables.

The TPO contacts are listed for each region to provide additional explanation or clarification.

Tony Johnson
Southern Research Station
USDA Forest Service
4700 Old Kingston Pike
Knoxville, TN 37919
tjohnson09@fs.fed.us
865-862-2042

Helen Beresford
Southern Research Station
USDA Forest Service
4700 Old Kingston Pike
Knoxville, TN 37919
hberesford@fs.fed.us
865-862-2091

James Bentley
Southern Research Station
USDA Forest Service
4700 Old Kingston Pike
Knoxville, TN 37919
jbentley@fs.fed.us
865-862-2056

Carolyn Steppleton
Southern Research Station
USDA Forest Service
200 W.T. Weaver Blvd.
Asheville, NC 28804
csteppleton@fs.fed.us
828-257-4848

# Contents

[a] All tables in this report are available in Microsoft® Excel workbook files. Upon request, these files will be supplied in the format the customer requests. The use of trade or firm names in this publication is for reader information and does not imply endorsement by the U.S. Department of Agriculture of any product or service.

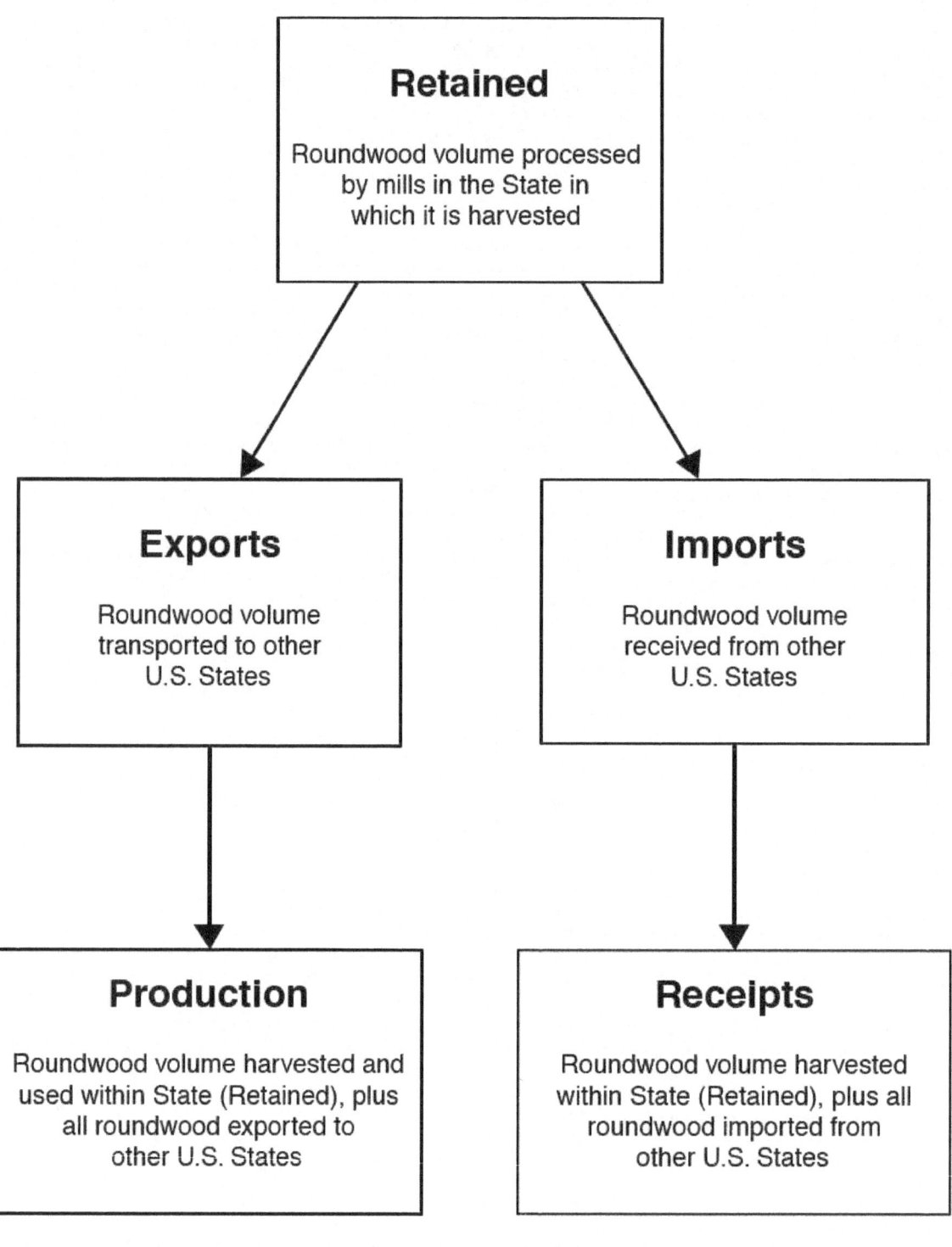

Figure 1—Movement of roundwood exports and imports within the United States.

# North Carolina's Timber Industry— An Assessment of Timber Product Output and Use, 2007

## Jason A. Cooper and Michael C. Mann

## Output of Industrial Timber Products

Note: Certain terms used in this report—retained, export, import, production, and receipts—have specialized meanings unique to the Forest Inventory and Analysis Units across the country that deal with timber product output (TPO) (fig. 1).

### All Products

- Between 2005 and 2007, TPO from roundwood was down 56 million cubic feet, or 7 percent, to 728 million cubic feet, while output of utilized plant byproducts was down 12 million cubic feet to 294 million cubic feet.

- Output of softwood roundwood products declined 8 percent to 474 million cubic feet, and the output of hardwood roundwood products declined 6 percent from 255 million cubic feet (fig. 2).

- Saw logs and pulpwood were the principal roundwood products in 2007. Combined output of these products totaled 629 million cubic feet and accounted for 86 percent of the State's total roundwood output (fig. 3).

- Total receipts at North Carolina mills, which included roundwood harvested and retained in the State as well as roundwood imported from other States, was down 37 million cubic feet to 714 million cubic feet. At the same time, the number of primary roundwood-using plants in North Carolina was down from 180 in 2005 to 163 in 2007 (fig. 4). Nearly all the decline was in sawmills.

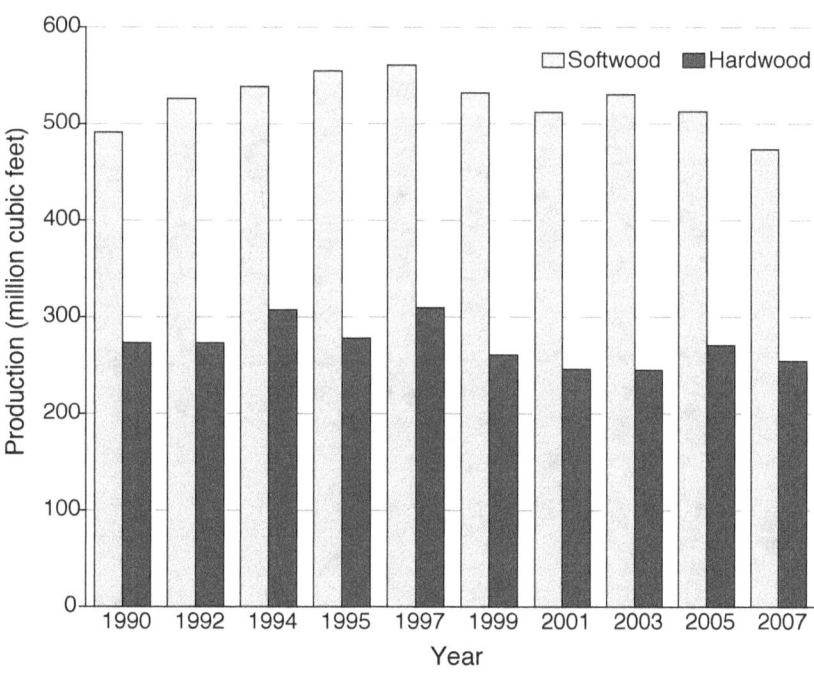

Figure 2—Roundwood production for all products by species group and year (see page 8 for references for individual years), North Carolina.

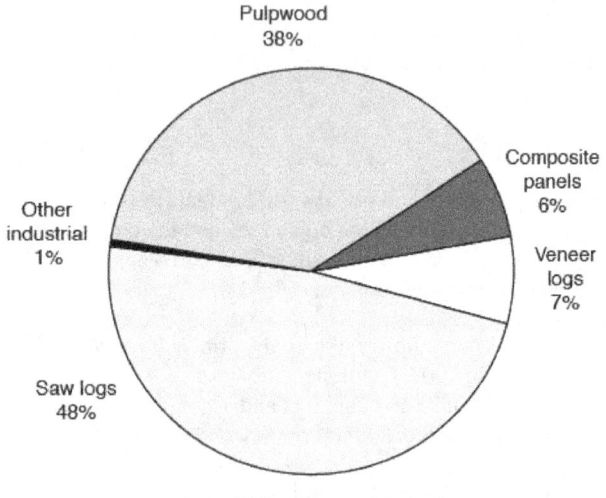

Total 728 million cubic feet

Figure 3—Roundwood production by type of product, North Carolina, 2007.

## Saw Logs

- Saw logs accounted for 48 percent of the State's total roundwood products. Output of softwood saw logs was down 15 percent to 245 million cubic feet (1.36 billion board feet, International ¼-inch rule), and the output of hardwood saw logs declined 6 percent to 104 million cubic feet (625 million board feet, International ¼-inch rule) (fig. 5).

- In 2007, North Carolina had 136 sawmills, a net loss of 17 mills since 2005. Total saw-log receipts were down about 40 million cubic feet to 374 million cubic feet but still accounted for 52 percent of the State's total receipts. Softwood saw-log receipts were down nearly 13 percent to 265 million cubic feet, while hardwood receipts declined slightly > 1 percent to 109 million cubic feet. Of the mills operating in 2007, 24 percent had receipts < 1 million board feet, while 40 percent had receipts > 10 million board feet. Those 55 mills accounted for 90 percent of saw-log receipts.

- North Carolina retained 94 percent of its saw-log production for within State manufacture. Saw-log imports at 46 million cubic feet exceeded exports by 26 million cubic feet in 2007, making the State a net importer of saw logs.

- Across all products, 83 percent of roundwood harvested was retained for processing at North Carolina mills. Exports of roundwood to other States amounted to 127 million cubic feet, while imports of roundwood amounted to 112 million cubic feet, making the State a net exporter of roundwood. Tables A.8 to A.12 show exports to and imports from other States by individual product type.

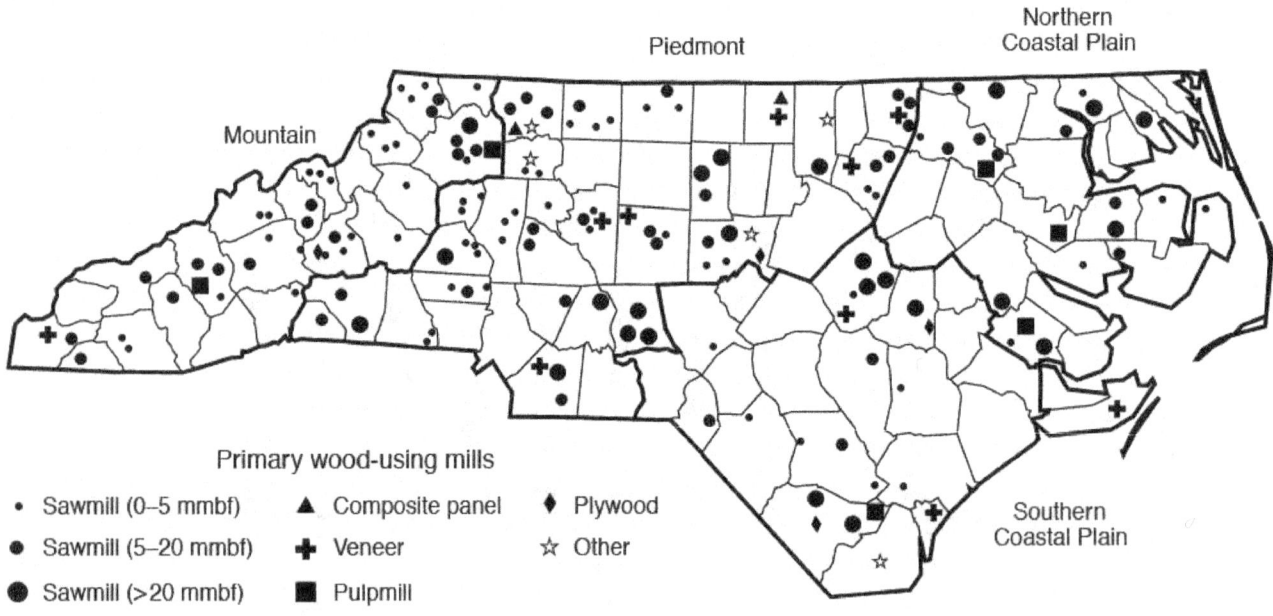

Primary wood-using mills

- Sawmill (0–5 mmbf)   ▲ Composite panel   ◆ Plywood
- Sawmill (5–20 mmbf)   ✚ Veneer   ☆ Other
- Sawmill (>20 mmbf)   ■ Pulpmill

Figure 4—Primary wood-using mills by region, North Carolina, 2007.

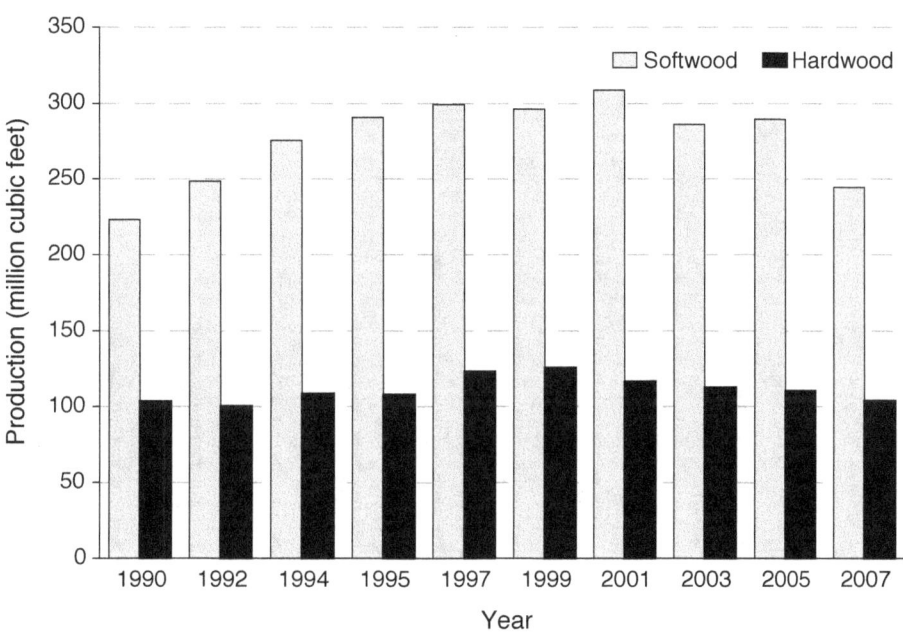

Figure 5—Roundwood saw-log production by species group and year (see page 8 for references for individual years), North Carolina.

## Pulpwood

- Pulpwood production, including chipped roundwood, increased 7 million cubic feet to 280 million cubic feet and accounted for 39 percent of the State's total roundwood TPO. Softwood output increased nearly 11 percent to 151 million cubic feet (2.1 million cords), while hardwood output decreased 6 percent to 129 million cubic feet (1.7 million cords) (fig. 6).

- Six pulpmill facilities were operating and receiving roundwood in North Carolina in 2007, the same as in 2005. Total pulpwood receipts for these mills were up 14 million cubic feet to 245 million cubic feet, accounting for 34 percent of total receipts for all mills.

- Seventy percent of roundwood cut for pulpwood was retained for processing by North Carolina pulpmills. Roundwood pulpwood accounted for 67 percent of total known exports and 44 percent of total imports. Roundwood pulpwood exports amounted to 85 million cubic feet, while imports totaled 50 million cubic feet, making the State a net exporter of roundwood pulpwood.

## Veneer Logs

- Output of veneer logs in 2007 totaled 50 million cubic feet and accounted for 7 percent of the State's total roundwood TPO volume. Softwood veneer production was down 19 percent to 36 million cubic feet (206 million board feet, International ¼-inch rule), and the output of hardwood veneer logs declined 6 percent to 14 million cubic feet (91 million board feet, International ¼-inch rule) (fig. 7).

- Fourteen veneer mills were operating in North Carolina in 2007, the same as in 2005. At the same time, receipts of veneer logs decreased 11 percent to 54 million cubic feet. Softwood veneer receipts were down 6.1 million cubic feet to 32 million cubic feet. Hardwood veneer receipts were down nearly 2 percent to 21 million cubic feet.

- North Carolina retained 85 percent of its veneer-log production for processing at veneer mills within the State. Imports amounted to 10.7 million cubic feet, while exports totaled 7.3 million cubic feet, making the State a net importer of roundwood veneer logs.

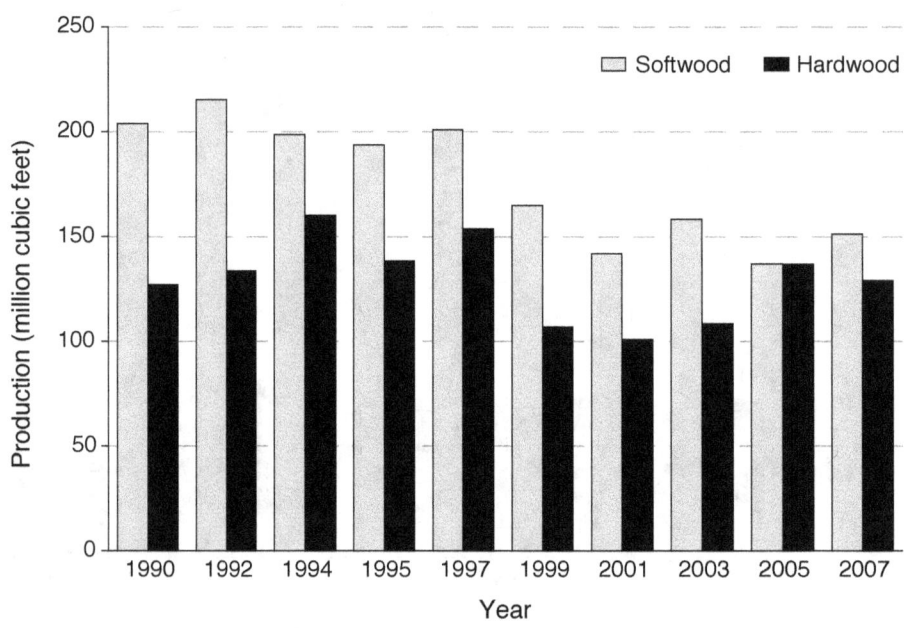

Figure 6—Roundwood pulpwood production by species group and year (see page 8 for references for individual years), North Carolina.

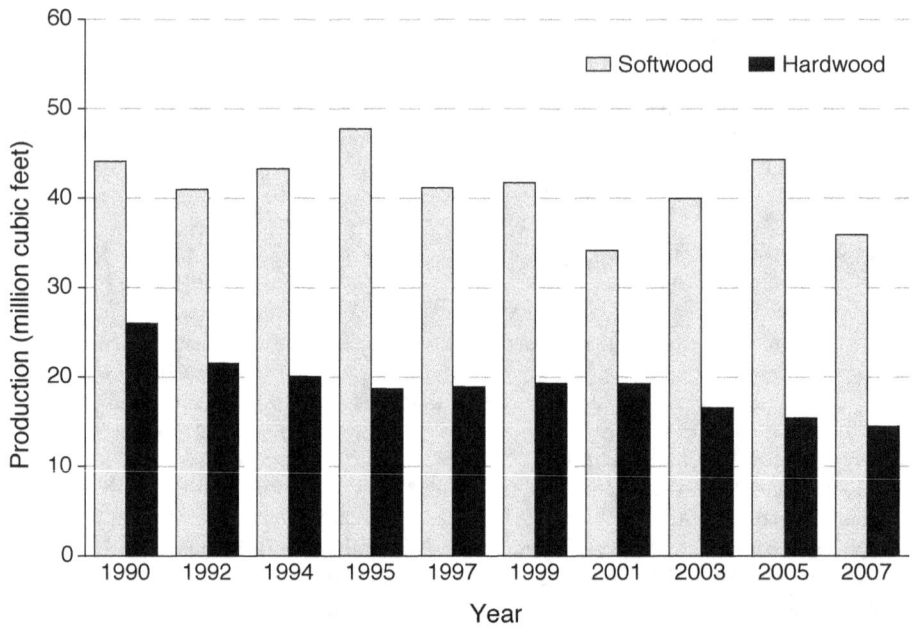

Figure 7—Roundwood veneer-log production by species group and year (see page 8 for references for individual years), North Carolina.

## Composite Panels

- Roundwood harvested from North Carolina's forests for composite panels declined 7 percent and totaled 46 million cubic feet. Softwood output was down 4 percent to 39 million cubic feet (543,000 cords), and hardwood output was down 23 percent to 6.4 million cubic feet (83,000 cords) (fig. 8).

- Two composite panel mills were operating in North Carolina in 2007, down from three in 2005. Total receipts for these mills decreased 12 percent to 40 million cubic feet.

- Seventy-three percent of the composite panel production was retained for processing by North Carolina mills. Exports amounted to 12.2 million cubic feet, while imports totaled 5.9 million cubic feet, making the State a net exporter of roundwood used for composite panels.

## Other Industrial Products

- Roundwood harvested for other industrial uses, e.g., poles, posts, mulch, firewood, logs for log homes, and all other industrial products, totaled 3.4 million cubic feet, up 136 percent from 2005. Softwood made up 70 percent of the other industrial products volume.

- The number of plants producing other industrial products increased from four in 2005 to five in 2007. Receipts of other industrial products totaled 1.3 million cubic feet.

- North Carolina was a net exporter of roundwood used for other industrial products. Of the 2 million cubic feet exported for other industrial uses, 52 percent was softwood.

## Plant Byproducts

- In 2007, processing of primary products in North Carolina mills generated 294 million cubic feet of wood and bark residues. Coarse residues from all primary products amounted to 128 million cubic feet, while bark volume totaled 69 million cubic feet. Sawdust and shavings made up 33 percent of total residues, or 98 million cubic feet (fig. 9).

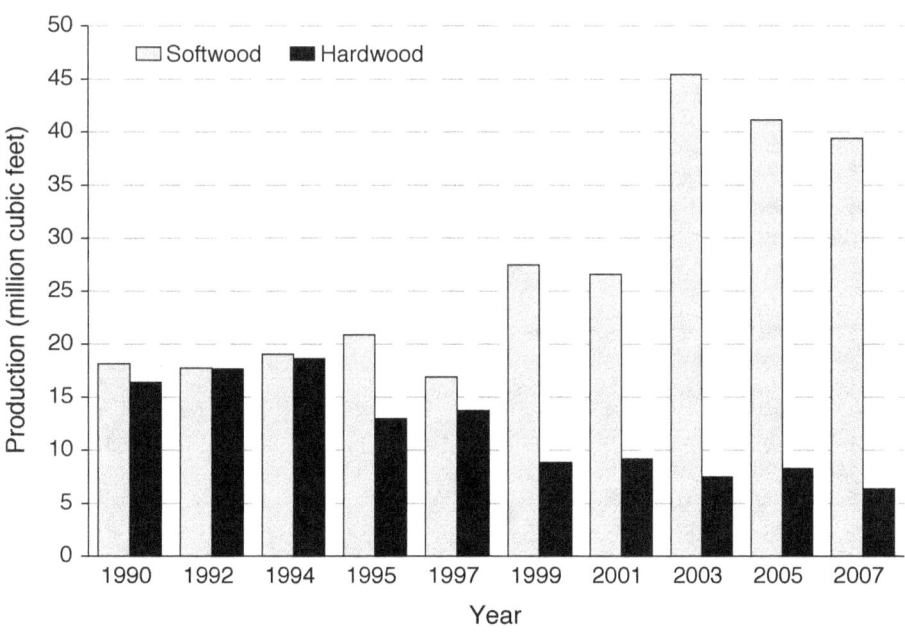

Figure 8—Roundwood production for composite panels by species group and year (see page 8 for references for individual years), North Carolina.

Figure 9—Primary mill residue by residue type, North Carolina, 2007.

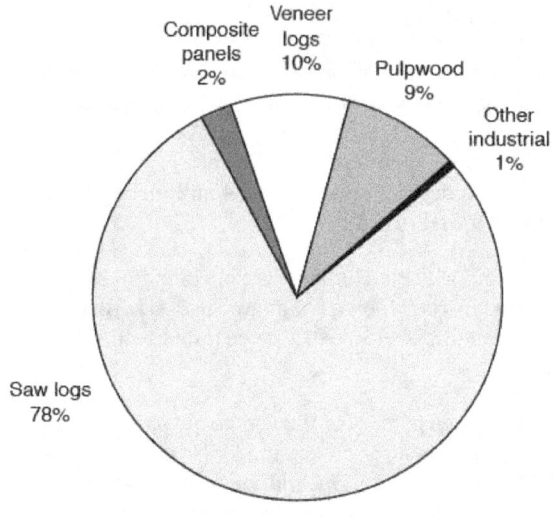

Figure 10—Disposal of residue by product, North Carolina, 2007.

- The processing of saw logs by sawmills generated 230 million cubic feet of mill residues, or 78 percent of the total residues produced (fig. 10).

- Less than 1 percent of the wood and bark residues were not used for a product, while 36 percent of the residues were used for industrial fuel (fig. 11). More than 107 million cubic feet, or 84 percent, of the coarse residues were used to manufacture fiber products. Most of the bark was used for industrial fuel or other miscellaneous products, while 78 percent of the sawdust and 10 percent of the shavings were used for industrial fuel. Shavings were used primarily for particleboard manufacture or miscellaneous uses such as bedding.

## County Data

- Table A.15 shows softwood and hardwood product output by county and individual product type. All 100 counties in North Carolina had softwood and hardwood output. Fourteen counties (Anson, Beaufort, Bertie, Bladen, Brunswick, Columbus, Craven, Halifax, Jones, Moore, Northampton, Onslow, Pitt, and Warren) had combined softwood and hardwood product output of >14 million cubic feet each. These 14 counties total product output amounted to 262 million cubic feet and accounted for 36 percent of the State's total product output.

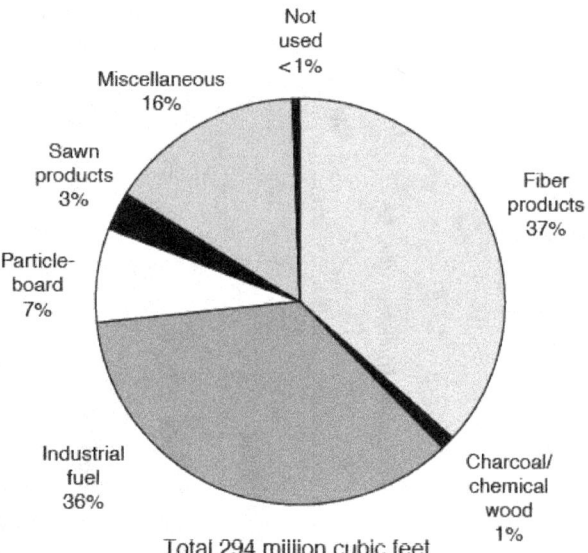

Figure 11—Primary mill residue produced by roundwood type, North Carolina, 2007.

## Total Roundwood Output

Using the most recent inventory data for North Carolina, product output by source, ownership, and detailed species group was estimated.

### Source

- In addition to the 728 million cubic feet of industrial roundwood output, an estimated 55 million cubic feet was harvested for domestic fuelwood, bringing North Carolina's total roundwood output to 783 million cubic feet.

- Ninety-seven percent of total roundwood output was considered growing-stock volume (sawtimber and poletimber) from timberland sources. Other sources (such as saplings; stumps, tops, and limbs of trees on timberland; and trees on nonforest land) contributed an estimated 22 million cubic feet, or 3 percent of total roundwood output (fig. 12).

### Ownership

- An estimated 653 million cubic feet, or 83 percent, of the total roundwood output came from nonindustrial private forest lands. Forest industry lands contributed 115 million cubic feet, or 15 percent of the output. Public lands made up the remaining 2 percent, or > 15 million cubic feet (fig. 13).

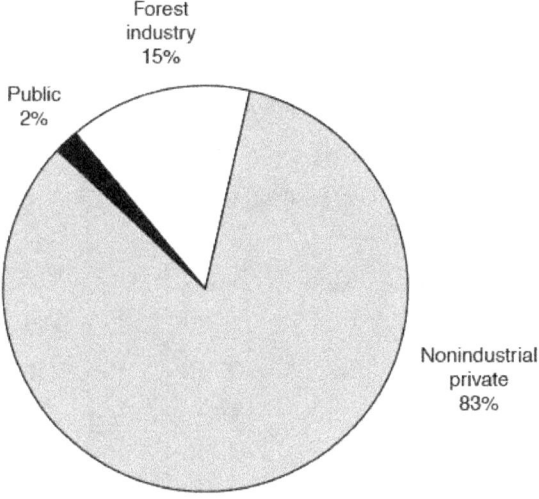

Total 783 million cubic feet

Figure 13—Roundwood output by ownership, North Carolina, 2007.

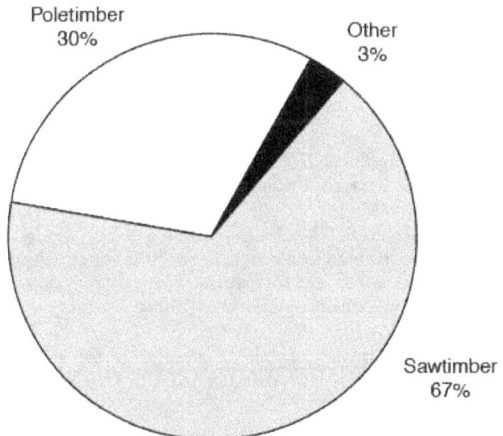

Total 783 million cubic feet

Figure 12—Roundwood output by source, North Carolina, 2007.

### Species

- The loblolly and shortleaf pine group provided the most volume of any softwood species group; at 383 million cubic feet, it accounted for 79 percent of the total softwood output (fig. 14). At 63 million cubic feet, other yellow pine types accounted for another 13 percent of softwood output. The red oak and white oak groups combined accounted for 112 million cubic feet, or 37 percent of total hardwood output (fig. 15).

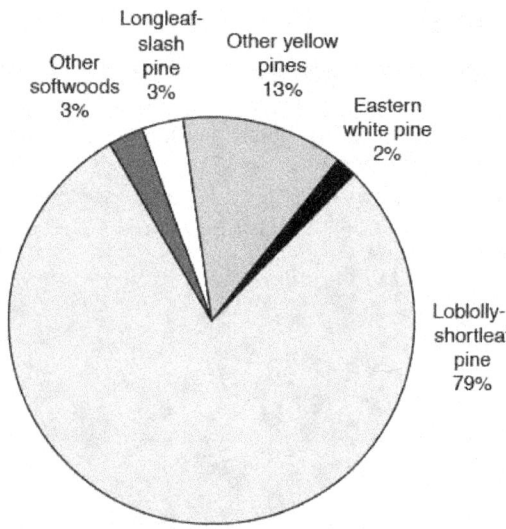

Total 483 million cubic feet

Figure 14—Roundwood output by softwood species group, North Carolina, 2007.

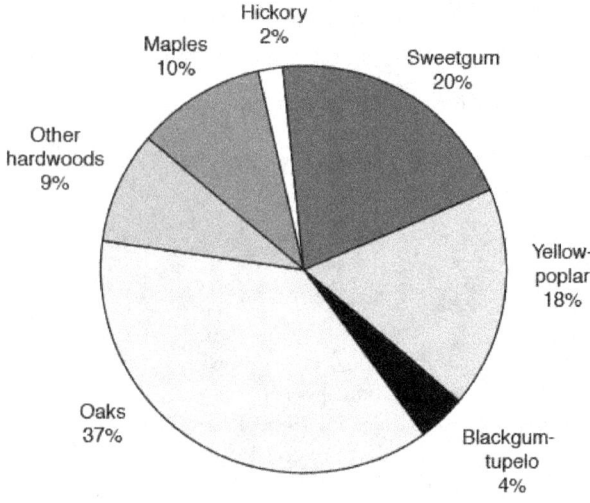

Total 301 million cubic feet

Figure 15—Roundwood output by hardwood species group, North Carolina, 2007.

## References

Davenport, E.L. 1992. Changes in North Carolina's industrial roundwood products output, 1987-1990. Resour. Bull. SE–132. Asheville, NC: U.S. Department of Agriculture Forest Service, Southeastern Forest Experiment Station. 22 p. [1990].

Howell, M.; Brown, D.R. 2004. North Carolina's timber industry—an assessment of timber product output and use, 2001. Resour. Bull. SRS–94. Asheville, NC: U.S. Department of Agriculture Forest Service, Southern Research Station. 39 p. [2001].

Howell, M.; New, B.D.; Mann, M.C. 2006. North Carolina's timber industry—an assessment of timber product output and use, 2003. Resour. Bull. SRS–112. Asheville, NC: U.S. Department of Agriculture Forest Service, Southern Research Station. 42 p. [2003].

Johnson, T.G. 1994. North Carolina's timber industry—an assessment of timber product output and use, 1992. Resour. Bull. SE–146. Asheville, NC: U.S. Department of Agriculture Forest Service, Southeastern Forest Experiment Station. 30 p. [1992].

Johnson, T.G.; Brown, D.R. 1996. North Carolina's timber industry—an assessment of timber product output and use, 1994. Resour. Bull. SRS–4. Asheville, NC: U.S. Department of Agriculture Forest Service, Southern Research Station. 31 p. [1994].

Johnson, T.G.; Brown, D.R. 1999. North Carolina's timber industry—an assessment of timber product output and use, 1997. Resour. Bull. SRS–39. Asheville, NC: U.S. Department of Agriculture Forest Service, Southern Research Station, 34 p. [1997].

Johnson, T.G.; Brown, D.R. 2002. North Carolina's timber industry—an assessment of timber product output and use, 1999. Resour. Bull. SRS–73. Asheville, NC: U.S. Department of Agriculture Forest Service, Southern Research Station. 39 p. [1999].

Johnson, T.G.; Jenkins, A.; Brown, D.R. 1997. North Carolina's timber industry—an assessment of timber product output and use, 1995. Resour. Bull. SRS–18. Asheville, NC: U.S. Department of Agriculture Forest Service, Southern Research Station. 35 p. [1995].

Johnson, T.G.; Mann, M.C. 2007. North Carolina's timber industry—an assessment of timber product output and use, 2005. Resour. Bull. SRS–127. Asheville, NC: U.S. Department of Agriculture Forest Service, Southern Research Station. 33 p. [2005].

Little, E.L., Jr. 1979. Checklist of United States trees (native and naturalized). Agric. Handb. 541. Washington, DC: U.S. Department of Agriculture. 375 p.

# Glossary

**Board foot.** A unit of measure applied to lumber that is 1-foot long, 1-foot wide, and 1-inch thick (or its equivalent) and also associated with roundwood as to its potential yield of such products.

**Byproducts.** Primary wood products, e.g., pulp chips, animal bedding, and fuelwood, recycled from mill residues.

**Composite panels.** Roundwood products manufactured into chips, wafers, strands, flakes, shavings, or sawdust and then reconstituted into a variety of panel and engineered lumber products.

**Consumption.** The quantity of a commodity, such as pulpwood, utilized by a particular mill or group of mills.

**Domestic fuelwood.** The volume of roundwood harvested to produce heat for residential settings.

**Drain.** The volume of roundwood removed from any geographic area where timber is grown.

**Exports.** The volume of domestic roundwood utilized by mills outside the State where timber was cut.

**Fiber products.** Byproducts used in the manufacture of pulp, paper, paperboard, and composite products, such as chipboard.

**Growing-stock removals.** The growing-stock volume removed from poletimber and sawtimber trees in the timberland inventory. (Note: Includes volume removed for roundwood products, logging residues, and other removals.)

**Growing-stock trees.** Living trees of commercial species classified as sawtimber, poletimber, saplings, and seedlings. Growing-stock trees must contain at least one 12-foot or two 8-foot logs in the saw-log portion, currently or potentially (if too small to qualify). The log(s) must meet dimension and merchantability standards and have, currently or potentially, one-third of the gross board-foot volume in sound wood.

**Growing-stock volume.** The cubic-foot volume of sound wood in growing-stock trees at least 5.0 inches d.b.h. from a 1-foot stump to a minimum 4.0-inch top d.o.b. of the central stem.

**Hardwoods.** Dicotyledonous trees, usually broadleaf and deciduous.

*Soft hardwoods.* Hardwood species with an average specific gravity of 0.50 or less, such as gums, yellow-poplar, cottonwoods, red maple, basswoods, and willows.

*Hard hardwoods.* Hardwood species with an average specific gravity >0.50, such as oaks, hard maples, hickories, and beech.

**Imports.** The volume of domestic roundwood delivered to a mill or group of mills in a specific State but harvested outside that State.

**Industrial fuelwood.** A roundwood product, with or without bark, used to generate energy at a manufacturing facility such as a wood-using mill.

**Industrial roundwood products.** Any primary use of the main stem of a tree, such as saw logs, pulpwood, veneer logs, intended to be processed into primary wood products such as lumber, wood pulp, sheathing, at primary wood-using mills.

**International ¼-inch rule.** A log rule or formula for estimating the board-foot volume of logs, allowing ½-inch of taper for each 4-foot length. The rule appears in a number of forms that allow for kerf. In the form used by FIA, a ¼-inch of kerf is assumed. This rule is used as the USDA Forest Service standard log rule in the Eastern United States.

**Log.** A primary forest product harvested in long, primarily 8-, 12-, and 16-foot lengths.

**Logging residues.** The unused merchantable portion of growing-stock trees cut or destroyed during logging operations.

**Merchantable portion.** That portion of live trees 5.0 inches d.b.h. and larger between a 1-foot stump and a minimum 4.0-inch top d.o.b. on the central stem. That portion of primary forks from the point of occurrence to a minimum 4.0-inch top d.o.b. is included.

**Merchantable volume.** Solid-wood volume in the merchantable portion of live trees.

**Noncommercial species.** Tree species of typically small size, poor form, or inferior quality that normally do not develop into trees suitable for industrial wood products.

**Nonforest land.** Land that has never supported forests and land formerly forested where timber production is precluded by development for other uses.

**Nongrowing-stock sources.** The net volume removed from the nongrowing-stock portions of poletimber and sawtimber trees (stumps, tops, limbs, cull sections of central stem) and from any portion of a rough, rotten, sapling, dead, or nonforest tree.

**Other forest land.** Forest land other than timberland and productive reserved forest land. It includes available and reserved forest land that is incapable of producing annually 20 cubic feet per acre of industrial wood under natural conditions because of adverse site conditions such as sterile soils, dry climate, poor drainage, high elevation, steepness, or rockiness.

**Other products.** A miscellaneous category of roundwood products, e.g., cooperage, excelsior, shingles, and mill residue byproducts (charcoal, bedding, mulch, etc.).

**Other removals.** The growing-stock volume of trees removed from the inventory by cultural operations such as timber stand improvement, land clearing, and other changes in land use, resulting in the removal of the trees from timberland.

**Other sources.** (See: Nongrowing-stock sources.)

**Ownership.** The property owned by one ownership unit, including all parcels of land in the United States.

*National forest land.* Federal land that has been legally designated as national forests or purchase units, and other land under the administration of the Forest Service, including experimental areas and Bankhead-Jones Title III land.

*Forest industry land.* Land owned by companies or individuals operating primary wood-using plants.

*Nonindustrial private forest (NIPF) land.* Privately owned land excluding forest industry land.

Corporate. Owned by corporations, including incorporated farm ownerships.

Individual. All lands owned by individuals, including farm operators.

*Other public.* An ownership class that includes all public lands except national forests.

Miscellaneous Federal land. Federal land other than national forests.

State, county, and municipal land. Land owned by States, counties, and local public agencies or municipalities, or land leased to these governmental units for 50 years or more.

**Plant residues.** Wood material generated in the production of timber products at primary manufacturing plants.

*Coarse residues.* Material, such as slabs, edgings, trim, veneer cores and ends, which is suitable for chipping.

*Fine residues.* Material, such as sawdust, shavings, and veneer residue, which is not suitable for chipping.

*Plant byproducts.* Residues (coarse or fine) used in the further manufacture of industrial products for consumer use, or as fuel.

*Unused plant residues.* Residues (coarse or fine) that are not used for any product, including fuel.

**Poletimber-size trees.** Softwoods 5.0 to 8.9 inches d.b.h. and hardwoods 5.0 to 10.9 inches d.b.h.

**Posts, poles, and pilings.** Roundwood products milled (cut or peeled) into standard sizes (lengths and circumferences) to be put in the ground to provide vertical and lateral support in buildings, foundations, utility lines, and fences. May also include nonindustrial (unmilled) products.

**Primary wood-using plants.** Industries that convert roundwood products (saw logs, veneer logs, pulpwood, etc.) into primary wood products, such as lumber, veneer or sheathing, wood pulp.

**Production.** The total volume of known roundwood harvested from land within a State, regardless of where it is consumed. Production is the sum of timber harvested and used within a State, and all roundwood exported to other States.

**Pulpwood.** A roundwood product that will be reduced to individual wood fibers by chemical or mechanical means. The fibers are used to make a broad generic group of pulp products that includes paper products, as well as fiberboard, insulating board, and paperboard.

10

**Receipts.** The quantity or volume of industrial roundwood received at a mill or by a group of mills in a State, regardless of the geographic source. Volume of roundwood receipts is equal to the volume of roundwood retained in a State plus roundwood imported from other States.

**Retained.** Roundwood volume harvested from and processed by mills within the same State.

**Rotten trees.** Live trees of commercial species not containing at least one 12-foot saw log, or two noncontiguous saw logs, each 8 feet or longer, now or prospectively, primarily because of rot or missing sections, and with less than one-third of the gross board-foot tree volume in sound material.

**Rough trees.** Live trees of commercial species not containing at least one 12-foot saw log, or two noncontiguous saw logs, each 8 feet or longer, now or prospectively, primarily because of roughness, poor form, splits, and cracks, and with less than one-third of the gross board-foot tree volume in sound material; and live trees of noncommercial species.

**Roundwood (roundwood logs).** Logs, bolts, or other round sections cut from trees for industrial manufacture or consumer uses.

**Roundwood chipped.** Any timber cut primarily for industrial manufacture, delivered to nonpulpmills, chipped, and then sold to pulpmills for use as fiber. Includes tops, jump sections, whole trees, and pulpwood sticks.

**Roundwood product drain.** That portion of total drain used for a product.

**Roundwood products.** Any primary product, such as lumber, veneer, composite panels, poles, pilings, pulp, or fuelwood that is produced from roundwood.

**Salvable dead trees.** Standing or downed dead trees that were formerly growing stock and considered merchantable. Trees must be at least 5.0 inches d.b.h. to qualify.

**Saplings.** Live trees 1.0 to 5.0 inches d.b.h.

**Saw log.** A roundwood product, usually 8 feet in length or longer, processed into a variety of sawn products such as lumber, cants, pallets, railroad ties, and timbers.

**Saw-log portion.** The part of the bole of sawtimber trees between a 1-foot stump and the saw-log top.

**Saw-log top.** The point on the bole of sawtimber trees above which a conventional saw log cannot be produced. The minimum saw-log top is 7.0 inches d.o.b. for softwoods and 9.0 inches d.o.b. for hardwoods for FIA standards.

**Sawtimber-size trees.** Softwoods 9.0 inches d.b.h. and larger and hardwoods 11.0 inches d.b.h. and larger.

**Sawtimber volume.** Growing-stock volume in the saw-log portion of sawtimber-sized trees in board feet (International ¼-inch rule).

**Seedlings.** Trees < 1.0 inch d.b.h. and > 1 foot tall for hardwoods, > 6 inches tall for softwoods, and > 0.5 inch in diameter at ground level for longleaf pine.

**Select red oaks.** A group of several red oak species composed of cherrybark, Shumard, and northern red oaks. Other red oak species are included in the "other red oaks" group.

**Select white oaks.** A group of several white oak species composed of white, swamp chestnut, swamp white, chinkapin, Durand, and bur oaks. Other white oak species are included in the "other white oaks" group.

**Softwoods.** Coniferous trees, usually evergreen, having leaves that are needles or scale like.

**Standard cord.** A unit of measure applied to roundwood, usually bolts or split wood. It is a stack of wood 4 feet high, 4 feet wide, and 8 feet long encompassing 128 cubic feet of wood, bark, and air space. This usually translates to approximately 75.0 to 81.0 cubic feet of solid wood for pulpwood, because pulpwood is more uniform.

**Standard unit.** A unit measure applied to roundwood timber products. Board feet (International ¼-inch rule) is the standard unit used for saw logs and veneer; cords are used for pulpwood, composite panel, and fuelwood; hundred pieces for poles; thousand pieces for posts; and thousand cubic feet for all other miscellaneous forest products.

**Timberland.** Forest land capable of producing 20 cubic feet of industrial wood per acre per year and not withdrawn from timber utilization.

**Timber product output.** The total volume of roundwood products from all sources plus the volume of byproducts recovered from mill residues (equals roundwood product drain).

**Timber products.** Roundwood products and byproducts.

**Timber removals.** The total volume of trees removed from the timberland inventory by harvesting, cultural operations such as stand improvement, land clearing, or changes in land use. (Note: Includes roundwood products, logging residues, and other removals.)

**Tree.** Woody plants having one erect perennial stem or trunk at least 3 inches d.b.h., a more or less definitely formed crown of foliage, and a height of at least 13 feet (at maturity).

**Upper-stem portion.** The part of the main stem of sawtimber trees above the saw-log top and the minimum top diameter of 4.0 inches outside bark, or to the point where the main stem breaks into limbs.

**Utilization studies.** Studies conducted on active logging operations to develop factors for merchantable portions of trees left in the woods (logging residues), logging damage, and utilization of the unmerchantable portion of growing-stock trees and nongrowing-stock trees.

**Veneer log.** A roundwood product either rotary cut, sliced, stamped, or sawn into a variety of veneer products such as plywood, finished panels, veneer sheets, or sheathing.

**Weight.** A unit of measure for mill residues, expressed as oven-dry tons (2,000 oven-dry pounds).

## Conversion Factors[a]

| | |
|---|---|
| **Saw logs** | |
| Softwood | 0.18018 cubic foot = 1 board foot |
| | 5.55 board feet = 1 cubic foot |
| Hardwood | 0.16556 cubic foot = 1 board foot |
| | 6.04 board feet = 1 cubic foot |
| **Veneer logs** | |
| Softwood | 0.17391 cubic foot = 1 board foot |
| | 5.75 board feet = 1 cubic foot |
| Hardwood | 0.15873 cubic foot = 1 board foot |
| | 6.30 board feet = 1 cubic foot |
| **Pulpwood**[b] | |
| Softwood | 72.5 cubic feet per cord |
| Hardwood | 76.6 cubic feet per cord |

[a] Conversion factors vary with stem size (d.b.h.) and species. The factors shown are for trees of average diameters removed in North Carolina during the most recent survey period.

[b] Cubic feet of solid wood per cord.

## Species List[a]

| Common name | Scientific name[b] | Common name | Scientific name[b] |
|---|---|---|---|
| **Softwoods** | | **Hardwoods (continued)** | |
| Atlantic white-cedar | *Chamaecyparis thyoides* (L.) B.S.P. | Kentucky coffeetree | *Gymnocladus dioicus* (L.) K. Koch |
| Southern redcedar | *Juniperus silicicola* (Small) Bailey | American holly | *Ilex opaca* Ait. |
| Eastern redcedar | *J. virginiana* L. | Black walnut | *Juglans nigra* L. |
| Shortleaf pine | *Pinus echinata* Mill. | Sweetgum | *Liquidambar styraciflua* L. |
| Longleaf pine | *P. palustris* Mill. | Yellow-poplar | *Liriodendron tulipifera* L. |
| Table Mt. pine | *P. pungens* Lamb. | Cucumbertree | *Magnolia acuminata* L. |
| Pitch pine | *P. rigida* Mill. | Southern magnolia | *M. grandiflora* L. |
| Pond pine | *P. serotina* Michx. | Bigleaf magnolia | *M. macrophylla* Michx. |
| Eastern white pine | *P. strobus* L. | Sweetbay | *M. virginiana* L. |
| Loblolly pine | *P. taeda* L. | Apple | *Malus* spp. Mill. |
| Virginia pine | *P. virginiana* Mill. | Chinaberry | *Melia azedarach* L. |
| Baldcypress | *Taxodium distichum* (L.) Rich. | White mulberry | *Morus alba* L. |
| Pond cypress | *Taxodium distichum* var. *nutans* (Ait.) Sweet | Red mulberry | *M. rubra* L. |
| | | Water tupelo | *Nyssa aquatica* L. |
| Eastern hemlock | *Tsuga canadensis* (L.) Carr. | Blackgum | *N. sylvatica* Marsh. |
| **Hardwoods** | | Swamp tupelo | *N. sylvatica* var. *biflora* (Walt.) Sarg. |
| Florida maple | *Acer barbatum* Michx. | Eastern hophornbeam | *Ostrya virginiana* (Mill.) K. Koch |
| Boxelder | *A. negundo* L. | Sourwood | *Oxydendrum arboreum* (L.) DC. |
| Red maple | *A. rubrum* L. | Redbay | *Persea borbonia* (L.) Spreng. |
| Silver maple | *A. saccharinum* L. | American sycamore | *Platanus occidentalis* L. |
| Sugar maple | *A. saccharum* Marsh. | Cottonwood | *Populus* spp. L. |
| Buckeye | *Aesculus* spp. L. | Black cherry | *Prunus serotina* Ehrh. |
| Yellow buckeye | *A. octandra* Marsh. | White oak | *Quercus alba* L. |
| Ailanthus | *Ailanthus altissima* (Mill.) Swingle | Scarlet oak | *Q. coccinea* Muenchh. |
| Serviceberry | *Amelanchier* spp. Medic. | Southern red oak | *Q. falcata* Michx. |
| River birch | *Betula nigra* L. | Cherrybark oak | *Q. falcata* var. *pagodifolia* Ell. |
| American hornbeam | *Carpinus caroliniana* Walt. | Bluejack oak | *Q. incana* Bartr. |
| Hickory | *Carya* spp. Nutt. | Turkey oak | *Q. laevis* Walt. |
| Water hickory | *C. aquatica* (Michx. f.) Nutt. | Laurel oak | *Q. laurifolia* Michx. |
| Bitternut hickory | *C. cordiformis* (Wangenh.) K. Koch | Overcup oak | *Q. lyrata* Walt. |
| Pignut hickory | *C. glabra* (Mill.) Sweet | Swamp chestnut oak | *Q. michauxii* Nutt. |
| Pecan | *C. illinoensis* (Wangenh.) K. Koch | Chinkapin oak | *Q. muehlenbergii* Engelm. |
| Shellbark hickory | *C. laciniosa* (Michx. f.) Loud. | Water oak | *Q. nigra* L. |
| Shagbark hickory | *C. ovata* (Mill.) K. Koch | Pin oak | *Q. palustris* Muenchh. |
| Mockernut hickory | *C. tomentosa* (Poir.) Nutt. | Willow oak | *Q. phellos* L. |
| Allegheny chinkapin | *Castanea pumila* Mill. | Chestnut oak | *Q. prinus* L. |
| Chinkapin | *Castanopsis* (D. Don) Spach | Northern red oak | *Q. rubra* L. |
| Catalpa | *Catalpa* spp. Scop. | Shumard oak | *Q. shumardii* Buckl. |
| Sugarberry | *Celtis laevigata* Willd. | Post oak | *Q. stellata* Wangenh. |
| Hackberry | *C. occidentalis* L. | Black oak | *Q. velutina* Lam. |
| Eastern redbud | *Cercis canadensis* L. | Live oak | *Q. virginiana* Mill. |
| Flowering dogwood | *Cornus florida* L. | Black locust | *Robinia pseudoacacia* L. |
| Hawthorn | *Crataegus* spp. L. | Willow | *Salix* spp. L. |
| Common persimmon | *Diospyros virginiana* L. | Sassafras | *Sassafras albidum* (Nutt.) Nees |
| American beech | *Fagus grandifolia* Ehrh. | American basswood | *Tilia americana* L. |
| White ash | *Fraxinus americana* L. | White basswood | *T. heterophylla* Vent. |
| Carolina ash | *F. caroliniana* Mill. | Winged elm | *Ulmus alata* Michx. |
| Green ash | *F. pennsylvanica* Marsh. | American elm | *U. americana* L. |
| Pumpkin ash | *F. profunda* (Bush) Bush | Slippery elm | *U. rubra* Muhl. |
| Waterlocust | *Gleditsia aquatica* Marsh. | Rock elm | *U. thomasii* Sarg. |
| Honeylocust | *G. triacanthos* L. | | |

[a] Common and scientific names of tree species ≥ 1.0 inch d.b h. occurring in the FIA sample.

[b] Little (1979).

# Appendix

## Index of Tables

**Table A.1—Output of industrial products by product and species group, North Carolina, 2005 and 2007**

| Product and species group | Year | | Change | Change |
|---|---|---|---|---|
| | 2005 | 2007 | | |
| | - - - - - thousand cubic feet - - - - - | | | percent |
| Saw logs | | | | |
| Softwood | 289,355 | 244,657 | -44,698 | -15.4 |
| Hardwood | 110,302 | 103,760 | -6,542 | -5.9 |
| Total | 399,657 | 348,417 | -51,240 | -12.8 |
| Veneer logs | | | | |
| Softwood | 44,337 | 35,911 | -8,426 | -19.0 |
| Hardwood | 15,437 | 14,505 | -932 | -6.0 |
| Total | 59,774 | 50,416 | -9,358 | -15.7 |
| Pulpwood[a] | | | | |
| Softwood | 136,936 | 151,350 | 14,414 | 10.5 |
| Hardwood | 136,726 | 129,059 | -7,667 | -5.6 |
| Total | 273,662 | 280,409 | 6,747 | 2.5 |
| Composite panels | | | | |
| Softwood | 41,126 | 39,403 | -1,723 | -4.2 |
| Hardwood | 8,271 | 6,356 | -1,915 | -23.2 |
| Total | 49,397 | 45,759 | -3,638 | -7.4 |
| Other industrial | | | | |
| Softwood | 1,408 | 2,383 | 975 | 69.2 |
| Hardwood | 22 | 1,000 | 978 | 4,445.5 |
| Total | 1,430 | 3,383 | 1,953 | 136.6 |
| All industrial | | | | |
| Softwood | 513,162 | 473,704 | -39,458 | -7.7 |
| Hardwood | 270,758 | 254,680 | -16,078 | -5.9 |
| Total | 783,920 | 728,384 | -55,536 | -7.1 |

[a] Includes roundwood delivered to nonpulpmills, then chipped and sold to pulpmills (7,051,000 cubic feet in 2005 and 4,608,000 cubic feet in 2007).

**Table A.2—Roundwood receipts by product and species group, North Carolina, 2005 and 2007**

| Product and species group | Year | | | |
|---|---|---|---|---|
| | 2005 | 2007 | Change | Change |
| | - - - - - *thousand cubic feet* - - - - - | | | *percent* |
| Saw logs | | | | |
| Softwood | 303,275 | 265,162 | -38,113 | -12.6 |
| Hardwood | 110,788 | 109,248 | -1,540 | -1.4 |
| Total | 414,063 | 374,410 | -39,653 | -9.6 |
| Veneer logs | | | | |
| Softwood | 38,491 | 32,347 | -6,144 | -16.0 |
| Hardwood | 21,765 | 21,441 | -324 | -1.5 |
| Total | 60,256 | 53,788 | -6,468 | -10.7 |
| Pulpwood[a] | | | | |
| Softwood | 139,970 | 155,112 | 15,142 | 10.8 |
| Hardwood | 91,355 | 89,950 | -1,405 | -1.5 |
| Total | 231,325 | 245,062 | 13,737 | 5.9 |
| Composite panels | | | | |
| Softwood | 38,304 | 32,838 | -5,466 | -14.3 |
| Hardwood | 6,521 | 6,673 | 152 | 2.3 |
| Total | 44,825 | 39,511 | -5,314 | -11.9 |
| Other industrial | | | | |
| Softwood | 883 | 1,302 | 419 | 47.5 |
| Hardwood | 0 | 0 | 0 | — |
| Total | 883 | 1,302 | 419 | 47.5 |
| Total output | | | | |
| Softwood | 520,923 | 486,761 | -34,162 | -6.6 |
| Hardwood | 230,429 | 227,312 | -3,117 | -1.4 |
| Total | 751,352 | 714,073 | -37,279 | -5.0 |

— = negligible.

[a] Includes roundwood delivered to nonpulpmills, then chipped and sold to pulpmills (9,658,000 cubic feet in 2005 and 5,933,000 cubic feet in 2007).

**Table A.3—Number of primary wood-using plants by type of mill, North Carolina, 1990 to 2007**

| Type of mill | Year | | | | | | | | | |
|---|---|---|---|---|---|---|---|---|---|---|
| | 1990 | 1992 | 1994 | 1995 | 1997 | 1999 | 2001 | 2003 | 2005 | 2007 |
| | *number* | | | | | | | | | |
| Sawmills | 308 | 306 | 275 | 273 | 243 | 240 | 215 | 204 | 153 | 136 |
| Veneer mills | 32 | 29 | 27 | 27 | 23 | 24 | 20 | 18 | 14 | 14 |
| Pulpmills | 8 | 8 | 8 | 8 | 7 | 7 | 7 | 6 | 6 | 6 |
| Composite panel mills | 5 | 4 | 4 | 4 | 3 | 3 | 3 | 3 | 3 | 2 |
| Other mills | 13 | 10 | 8 | 8 | 4 | 4 | 4 | 4 | 4 | 5 |
| All plants | 366 | 357 | 322 | 320 | 280 | 278 | 249 | 235 | 180 | 163 |

**Table A.4—Roundwood receipts by sawmill size, North Carolina, 2005 and 2007**

| Sawmill size class[a] | 2005 | | | 2007 | | |
|---|---|---|---|---|---|---|
| | Mills | Volume | | Mills | Volume | |
| *mmbf* | *number* | *mbf* | *percent* | *number* | *mbf* | *percent* |
| <1.0 | 37 | 12,317 | 1 | 32 | 12,234 | 1 |
| 1.0–4.99 | 41 | 106,536 | 4 | 34 | 87,200 | 4 |
| 5.0–9.99 | 17 | 116,556 | 5 | 15 | 103,618 | 5 |
| 10.0–49.99 | 45 | 827,473 | 35 | 44 | 836,201 | 39 |
| >50 | 13 | 1,289,790 | 55 | 11 | 1,092,535 | 51 |
| Total | 153 | 2,352,672 | 100 | 136 | 2,131,788 | 100 |

[a] Based on volume received as opposed to actual capacity.

**Table A.5—Roundwood receipts by species and type of mill, North Carolina, 2007**

| Species | All mills | Sawmills | Veneer mills Pine plywood | Veneer mills Other veneer | OSB and panels | Pulpmills[a] | Other mills |
|---|---|---|---|---|---|---|---|
| | | | *thousand cubic feet* | | | | |
| Softwood | | | | | | | |
| Yellow pine | 311,579 | 245,856 | 32,265 | 75 | 32,081 | NA | 1,302 |
| Eastern white pine | 15,672 | 14,915 | 0 | 0 | 757 | NA | 0 |
| Cedar | 296 | 289 | 0 | 7 | 0 | NA | 0 |
| Cypress | 3,754 | 3,754 | 0 | 0 | 0 | NA | 0 |
| Other softwood | 348 | 348 | 0 | 0 | 0 | NA | 0 |
| Unclassified | 155,112 | 0 | 0 | 0 | 0 | 155,112 | 0 |
| Total softwoods | 486,761 | 265,162 | 32,265 | 82 | 32,838 | 155,112 | 1,302 |
| Hardwood | | | | | | | |
| Blackgum-tupelo | 3,920 | 2,142 | 568 | 812 | 398 | NA | 0 |
| Soft maple | 7,417 | 5,542 | 63 | 4 | 1,808 | NA | 0 |
| Sweetgum | 13,376 | 8,079 | 3,268 | 1,005 | 1,024 | NA | 0 |
| Yellow-poplar | 53,183 | 35,833 | 9,655 | 4,650 | 3,045 | NA | 0 |
| Other soft hardwood | 1,312 | 773 | 141 | 0 | 398 | NA | 0 |
| Hickory | 3,519 | 3,485 | 0 | 34 | 0 | NA | 0 |
| Red oak | 24,349 | 24,081 | 0 | 268 | 0 | NA | 0 |
| White oak | 21,205 | 20,889 | 0 | 316 | 0 | NA | 0 |
| Other hard hardwood | 9,081 | 8,424 | 0 | 657 | 0 | NA | 0 |
| Unclassified | 90,034 | 0 | 0 | 0 | 0 | 90,034 | 0 |
| Total hardwoods | 227,396 | 109,248 | 13,695 | 7,746 | 6,673 | 90,034 | 0 |
| All species | 714,157 | 374,410 | 45,960 | 7,828 | 39,511 | 245,146 | 1,302 |

NA = not applicable; OSB = oriented strand board.

[a] Collected only by softwood and hardwood and includes roundwood chipped.

**Table A.6—Industrial roundwood movement by year and species group, North Carolina, 2005 and 2007**

| Year | Production | Exported to other States | Retained | Imported from other States | Receipts |
|---|---|---|---|---|---|
| | | *thousand cubic feet* | | | |
| **Softwood** | | | | | |
| 2005 | 513,162 | 76,200 | 436,962 | 83,961 | 520,923 |
| 2007 | 473,704 | 64,792 | 408,912 | 77,849 | 486,761 |
| **Hardwood** | | | | | |
| 2005 | 270,758 | 70,538 | 200,220 | 30,209 | 230,429 |
| 2007 | 254,680 | 61,898 | 192,782 | 34,530 | 227,312 |
| **All species** | | | | | |
| 2005 | 783,920 | 146,738 | 637,182 | 114,170 | 751,352 |
| 2007 | 728,384 | 126,690 | 601,694 | 112,379 | 714,073 |

**Table A.7—Industrial roundwood movement by product and species group, North Carolina, 2007**

| Product and species group | Production | Exported to other States | Retained | Imported from other States | Receipts |
|---|---|---|---|---|---|
| | | | *thousand cubic feet* | | |
| **Saw logs** | | | | | |
| Softwood | 244,657 | 13,470 | 231,187 | 33,975 | 265,162 |
| Hardwood | 103,760 | 6,577 | 97,183 | 12,065 | 109,248 |
| Total | 348,417 | 20,047 | 328,370 | 46,040 | 374,410 |
| **Veneer logs** | | | | | |
| Softwood | 35,911 | 6,761 | 29,150 | 3,197 | 32,347 |
| Hardwood | 14,505 | 566 | 13,939 | 7,502 | 21,441 |
| Total | 50,416 | 7,327 | 43,089 | 10,699 | 53,788 |
| **Pulpwood**[a] | | | | | |
| Softwood | 151,350 | 31,987 | 119,363 | 35,749 | 155,112 |
| Hardwood | 129,059 | 53,078 | 75,981 | 13,969 | 89,950 |
| Total | 280,409 | 85,065 | 195,344 | 49,718 | 245,062 |
| **Composite panels** | | | | | |
| Softwood | 39,403 | 11,493 | 27,910 | 4,928 | 32,838 |
| Hardwood | 6,356 | 677 | 5,679 | 994 | 6,673 |
| Total | 45,759 | 12,170 | 33,589 | 5,922 | 39,511 |
| **Other industrial** | | | | | |
| Softwood | 2,383 | 1,081 | 1,302 | 0 | 1,302 |
| Hardwood | 1,000 | 1,000 | 0 | 0 | 0 |
| Total | 3,383 | 2,081 | 1,302 | 0 | 1,302 |
| **All products** | | | | | |
| Softwood | 473,704 | 64,792 | 408,912 | 77,849 | 486,761 |
| Hardwood | 254,680 | 61,898 | 192,782 | 34,530 | 227,312 |
| Total | 728,384 | 126,690 | 601,694 | 112,379 | 714,073 |

[a] Includes roundwood delivered to nonpulpmills, then chipped and sold to pulpmills.

Table A.8—Saw-log volume by destination, source, and species group, North Carolina, 2007

| Destination and source | All species | Species group | |
| --- | --- | --- | --- |
| | | Softwood | Hardwood |
| | *thousand cubic feet* | | |
| North Carolina (retained) | 328,370 | 231,187 | 97,183 |
| Exports to | | | |
| Georgia | 139 | 126 | 13 |
| Kentucky | 3 | 3 | 0 |
| South Carolina | 2,452 | 2,135 | 317 |
| Tennessee | 1,351 | 493 | 858 |
| Virginia | 16,102 | 10,713 | 5,389 |
| Total | 20,047 | 13,470 | 6,577 |
| Imports from | | | |
| Georgia | 1,139 | 39 | 1,100 |
| South Carolina | 20,770 | 15,826 | 4,944 |
| Tennessee | 1,059 | 97 | 962 |
| Virginia | 23,072 | 18,013 | 5,059 |
| Total | 46,040 | 33,975 | 12,065 |

Table A.9—Veneer volume by destination, source, and species group, North Carolina, 2007

| Destination and source | All species | Species group | |
| --- | --- | --- | --- |
| | | Softwood | Hardwood |
| | *thousand cubic feet* | | |
| North Carolina (retained) | 43,089 | 29,150 | 13,939 |
| Exports to | | | |
| Georgia | 512 | 332 | 180 |
| South Carolina | 2,823 | 2,551 | 272 |
| Virginia | 3,992 | 3,878 | 114 |
| Total | 7,327 | 6,761 | 566 |
| Imports from | | | |
| Georgia | 185 | 15 | 170 |
| Indiana | 38 | 0 | 38 |
| Kentucky | 1,776 | 0 | 1,776 |
| New York | 154 | 0 | 154 |
| Ohio | 140 | 0 | 140 |
| Pennsylvania | 804 | 0 | 804 |
| South Carolina | 3,462 | 3,174 | 288 |
| Tennessee | 1,315 | 0 | 1,315 |
| Virginia | 2,817 | 0 | 2,817 |
| West Virginia | 8 | 8 | 0 |
| Total | 10,699 | 3,197 | 7,502 |

**Table A.10—Pulpwood volume by destination, source, and species group, North Carolina, 2007[a]**

| Destination and source | All species | Species group | |
|---|---|---|---|
| | | Softwood | Hardwood |
| | *thousand cubic feet* | | |
| North Carolina (retained) | 195,344 | 119,363 | 75,981 |
| Exports to | | | |
| Georgia | 37 | 0 | 37 |
| Kentucky | 85 | 0 | 85 |
| South Carolina | 41,534 | 24,321 | 17,213 |
| Tennessee | 7,825 | 1,181 | 6,644 |
| Virginia | 35,584 | 6,485 | 29,099 |
| Total | 85,065 | 31,987 | 53,078 |
| Imports from | | | |
| Alabama | 145 | 0 | 145 |
| Georgia | 469 | 143 | 326 |
| South Carolina | 26,047 | 21,783 | 4,264 |
| Tennessee | 7,891 | 1 | 7,890 |
| Virginia | 15,166 | 13,822 | 1,344 |
| Total | 49,718 | 35,749 | 13,969 |

[a] Includes roundwood delivered to nonpulpmills, then chipped and sold to pulpmills.

**Table A.11—Composite panel volume by destination, source, and species group, North Carolina, 2007**

| Destination and source | All species | Species group | |
|---|---|---|---|
| | | Softwood | Hardwood |
| | *thousand cubic feet* | | |
| North Carolina (retained) | 33,589 | 27,910 | 5,679 |
| Exports to | | | |
| Virginia | 12,170 | 11,493 | 677 |
| Total | 12,170 | 11,493 | 677 |
| Imports from | | | |
| Virginia | 5,922 | 4,928 | 994 |
| Total | 5,922 | 4,928 | 994 |

**Table A.12—Other industrial volume by destination, source, and species group, North Carolina, 2007[a]**

| Destination and source | All species | Species group | |
|---|---|---|---|
| | | Softwood | Hardwood |
| | *thousand cubic feet* | | |
| North Carolina (retained) | 1,302 | 1,302 | 0 |
| Exports to | | | |
| South Carolina | 60 | 60 | 0 |
| Virginia | 2,021 | 1,021 | 1,000 |
| Total | 2,081 | 1,081 | 1,000 |

[a] Includes poles, posts, mulch, firewood, log homes, charcoal, and all other industrial mills.

**Table A.13—Primary mill residue volume by roundwood type, species group, and residue type, North Carolina, 2007**

| Roundwood type and species group | All types | Residue type | | | |
|---|---|---|---|---|---|
| | | Bark | Coarse | Sawdust | Shavings |
| | | *thousand cubic feet* | | | |
| Saw logs | | | | | |
| Softwood | 165,810 | 17,801 | 78,492 | 47,148 | 22,369 |
| Hardwood | 64,402 | 11,318 | 30,702 | 21,868 | 514 |
| Total | 230,212 | 29,119 | 109,194 | 69,016 | 22,883 |
| Veneer logs | | | | | |
| Softwood | 17,017 | 2,247 | 11,048 | 3,722 | 0 |
| Hardwood | 11,327 | 2,324 | 7,082 | 1,921 | 0 |
| Total | 28,344 | 4,571 | 18,130 | 5,643 | 0 |
| Pulpwood | | | | | |
| Softwood | 15,482 | 15,482 | 0 | 0 | 0 |
| Hardwood | 11,286 | 11,286 | 0 | 0 | 0 |
| Total | 26,768 | 26,768 | 0 | 0 | 0 |
| Composite panels | | | | | |
| Softwood | 5,468 | 5,468 | 0 | 0 | 0 |
| Hardwood | 1,503 | 1,503 | 0 | 0 | 0 |
| Total | 6,971 | 6,971 | 0 | 0 | 0 |
| Other industrial[a] | | | | | |
| Softwood | 1,529 | 1,273 | 256 | 0 | 0 |
| Hardwood | 0 | 0 | 0 | 0 | 0 |
| Total | 1,529 | 1,273 | 256 | 0 | 0 |
| Total | | | | | |
| Softwood | 205,306 | 42,271 | 89,796 | 50,870 | 22,369 |
| Hardwood | 88,518 | 26,431 | 37,784 | 23,789 | 514 |
| Total | 293,824 | 68,702 | 127,580 | 74,659 | 22,883 |

[a] Includes poles, pilings, posts, and all other industrial products.

**Table A.14—Disposal of residue at primary wood-using plants by product, species group, and type of residue, North Carolina, 2005 and 2007**

| Product and species group | All types 2005 | All types 2007 | Bark 2005 | Bark 2007 | Coarse 2005 | Coarse 2007 | Sawdust 2005 | Sawdust 2007 | Shavings 2005 | Shavings 2007 |
|---|---|---|---|---|---|---|---|---|---|---|
| | | | | | *thousand cubic feet* | | | | | |
| **Fiber products** | | | | | | | | | | |
| Softwood | 84,994 | 78,346 | 0 | 0 | 84,031 | 77,853 | 963 | 493 | 0 | 0 |
| Hardwood | 31,395 | 29,969 | 29 | 0 | 31,309 | 29,912 | 57 | 57 | 0 | 0 |
| Total | 116,389 | 108,315 | 29 | 0 | 115,340 | 107,765 | 1,020 | 550 | 0 | 0 |
| **Particleboard** | | | | | | | | | | |
| Softwood | 14,327 | 19,989 | 3 | 50 | 3,729 | 5,199 | 3,093 | 5,626 | 7,502 | 9,114 |
| Hardwood | 2,416 | 2,134 | 35 | 55 | 1,621 | 1,861 | 592 | 218 | 168 | 0 |
| Total | 16,743 | 22,123 | 38 | 105 | 5,350 | 7,060 | 3,685 | 5,844 | 7,670 | 9,114 |
| **Charcoal/ chemical wood** | | | | | | | | | | |
| Softwood | 3,178 | 2,780 | 0 | 0 | 0 | 0 | 3,178 | 2,780 | 0 | 0 |
| Hardwood | 0 | 0 | 0 | 0 | 0 | 0 | 0 | 0 | 0 | 0 |
| Total | 3,178 | 2,780 | 0 | 0 | 0 | 0 | 3,178 | 2,780 | 0 | 0 |
| **Sawn products** | | | | | | | | | | |
| Softwood | 2,790 | 5,364 | 0 | 0 | 2,790 | 5,364 | 0 | 0 | 0 | 0 |
| Hardwood | 54 | 3,436 | 0 | 1 | 54 | 3,435 | 0 | 0 | 0 | 0 |
| Total | 2,844 | 8,800 | 0 | 1 | 2,844 | 8,799 | 0 | 0 | 0 | 0 |
| **Industrial fuel** | | | | | | | | | | |
| Softwood | 71,736 | 66,139 | 25,495 | 26,609 | 212 | 334 | 44,226 | 37,347 | 1,803 | 1,849 |
| Hardwood | 39,439 | 39,054 | 15,862 | 16,007 | 2,038 | 1,615 | 21,244 | 21,024 | 295 | 408 |
| Total | 111,175 | 105,193 | 41,357 | 42,616 | 2,250 | 1,949 | 65,470 | 58,371 | 2,098 | 2,257 |
| **Miscellaneous** | | | | | | | | | | |
| Softwood | 41,433 | 32,598 | 17,984 | 15,606 | 1,153 | 1,015 | 6,164 | 4,571 | 16,132 | 11,406 |
| Hardwood | 13,780 | 13,709 | 10,892 | 10,351 | 963 | 946 | 1,767 | 2,306 | 158 | 106 |
| Total | 55,213 | 46,307 | 28,876 | 25,957 | 2,116 | 1,961 | 7,931 | 6,877 | 16,290 | 11,512 |
| **Not used** | | | | | | | | | | |
| Softwood | 714 | 90 | 11 | 6 | 45 | 31 | 658 | 53 | 0 | 0 |
| Hardwood | 536 | 216 | 14 | 17 | 37 | 15 | 485 | 184 | 0 | 0 |
| Total | 1,250 | 306 | 25 | 23 | 82 | 46 | 1,143 | 237 | 0 | 0 |
| **All products** | | | | | | | | | | |
| Softwood | 219,172 | 205,306 | 43,493 | 42,271 | 91,960 | 89,796 | 58,282 | 50,870 | 25,437 | 22,369 |
| Hardwood | 87,620 | 88,518 | 26,832 | 26,431 | 36,022 | 37,784 | 24,145 | 23,789 | 621 | 514 |
| Total | 306,792 | 293,824 | 70,325 | 68,702 | 127,982 | 127,580 | 82,427 | 74,659 | 26,058 | 22,883 |

**Table A.15—Roundwood timber product output by county, product, and species group, North Carolina, 2007**

| County | All products Soft-wood | Hard-wood | Saw logs Soft-wood | Hard-wood | Veneer logs Soft-wood | Hard-wood | Pulpwood[a] Soft-wood | Hard-wood | Composite panels Soft-wood | Hard-wood | Other industrial Soft-wood | Hard-wood |
|---|---|---|---|---|---|---|---|---|---|---|---|---|
| | | | | | *thousand cubic feet* | | | | | | | |
| Alamance | 3,639 | 2,607 | 3,032 | 1,961 | 0 | 0 | 42 | 646 | 565 | 0 | 0 | 0 |
| Alexander | 1,464 | 931 | 1,182 | 741 | 0 | 0 | 2 | 139 | 280 | 51 | 0 | 0 |
| Alleghany | 625 | 1,433 | 620 | 880 | 0 | 0 | 5 | 502 | 0 | 51 | 0 | 0 |
| Anson | 12,085 | 1,922 | 5,597 | 1,045 | 842 | 0 | 5,646 | 877 | 0 | 0 | 0 | 0 |
| Ashe | 1,389 | 3,010 | 1,307 | 2,471 | 0 | 0 | 82 | 539 | 0 | 0 | 0 | 0 |
| Avery | 146 | 1,292 | 146 | 1,222 | 0 | 70 | 0 | 0 | 0 | 0 | 0 | 0 |
| Beaufort | 32,770 | 5,385 | 25,245 | 611 | 0 | 208 | 7,525 | 4,566 | 0 | 0 | 0 | 0 |
| Bertie | 17,548 | 5,110 | 8,604 | 1,149 | 0 | 702 | 8,577 | 3,246 | 332 | 13 | 35 | 0 |
| Bladen | 12,404 | 2,361 | 6,011 | 1,056 | 1,415 | 84 | 4,880 | 1,221 | 0 | 0 | 98 | 0 |
| Brunswick | 18,092 | 1,298 | 8,192 | 73 | 2,831 | 81 | 6,989 | 1,144 | 0 | 0 | 80 | 0 |
| Buncombe | 602 | 2,066 | 280 | 1,373 | 0 | 283 | 322 | 410 | 0 | 0 | 0 | 0 |
| Burke | 3,165 | 2,379 | 1,378 | 962 | 0 | 0 | 806 | 1,417 | 981 | 0 | 0 | 0 |
| Cabarrus | 1,275 | 540 | 697 | 472 | 0 | 0 | 438 | 17 | 140 | 51 | 0 | 0 |
| Caldwell | 1,711 | 1,878 | 1,675 | 1,647 | 0 | 20 | 36 | 160 | 0 | 51 | 0 | 0 |
| Camden | 1,290 | 3,413 | 491 | 575 | 0 | 407 | 355 | 2,425 | 415 | 6 | 29 | 0 |
| Carteret | 4,112 | 649 | 2,020 | 37 | 0 | 0 | 2,092 | 612 | 0 | 0 | 0 | 0 |
| Caswell | 7,115 | 3,486 | 2,298 | 1,113 | 0 | 175 | 30 | 1,667 | 4,787 | 531 | 0 | 0 |
| Catawba | 2,287 | 1,209 | 1,676 | 1,085 | 0 | 70 | 51 | 54 | 560 | 0 | 0 | 0 |
| Chatham | 8,405 | 3,683 | 5,943 | 3,119 | 0 | 178 | 191 | 386 | 2,072 | 0 | 199 | 0 |
| Cherokee | 1,946 | 3,442 | 138 | 1,144 | 332 | 189 | 1,476 | 2,109 | 0 | 0 | 0 | 0 |
| Chowan | 1,782 | 781 | 849 | 7 | 0 | 0 | 904 | 774 | 0 | 0 | 29 | 0 |
| Clay | 483 | 869 | 26 | 314 | 0 | 8 | 457 | 547 | 0 | 0 | 0 | 0 |
| Cleveland | 3,008 | 1,991 | 1,486 | 1,461 | 0 | 12 | 962 | 467 | 560 | 51 | 0 | 0 |
| Columbus | 17,988 | 3,025 | 9,043 | 899 | 2,973 | 201 | 5,745 | 1,925 | 0 | 0 | 227 | 0 |
| Craven | 19,516 | 3,221 | 12,619 | 0 | 1,268 | 239 | 5,629 | 2,982 | 0 | 0 | 0 | 0 |
| Cumberland | 2,095 | 1,710 | 478 | 136 | 283 | 410 | 1,334 | 1,164 | 0 | 0 | 0 | 0 |
| Currituck | 794 | 627 | 532 | 194 | 0 | 0 | 227 | 433 | 0 | 0 | 35 | 0 |
| Dare | 283 | 13 | 280 | 0 | 0 | 0 | 3 | 13 | 0 | 0 | 0 | 0 |
| Davidson | 1,599 | 2,290 | 861 | 1,875 | 0 | 65 | 38 | 194 | 700 | 156 | 0 | 0 |
| Davie | 389 | 689 | 239 | 546 | 0 | 0 | 6 | 143 | 140 | 0 | 4 | 0 |
| Duplin | 6,742 | 3,367 | 2,002 | 106 | 2,095 | 350 | 2,645 | 2,911 | 0 | 0 | 0 | 0 |
| Durham | 2,383 | 597 | 1,630 | 339 | 0 | 5 | 0 | 253 | 753 | 0 | 0 | 0 |
| Edgecombe | 6,694 | 2,936 | 2,472 | 609 | 1,087 | 335 | 2,803 | 1,979 | 332 | 13 | 0 | 0 |
| Forsyth | 1,197 | 1,803 | 862 | 1,435 | 0 | 0 | 55 | 212 | 280 | 156 | 0 | 0 |
| Franklin | 5,620 | 3,111 | 2,573 | 1,055 | 514 | 124 | 963 | 1,756 | 1,480 | 46 | 90 | 130 |
| Gaston | 2,731 | 970 | 1,363 | 376 | 842 | 0 | 232 | 491 | 280 | 103 | 14 | 0 |
| Gates | 9,176 | 4,464 | 3,957 | 1,241 | 14 | 46 | 4,623 | 3,085 | 582 | 92 | 0 | 0 |
| Graham | 1 | 1,081 | 1 | 47 | 0 | 433 | 0 | 601 | 0 | 0 | 0 | 0 |
| Granville | 7,403 | 4,152 | 3,623 | 1,083 | 20 | 199 | 43 | 2,272 | 3,538 | 598 | 179 | 0 |
| Greene | 1,372 | 1,190 | 782 | 179 | 0 | 17 | 402 | 723 | 0 | 0 | 188 | 271 |
| Guilford | 856 | 2,971 | 466 | 2,480 | 0 | 0 | 61 | 318 | 280 | 103 | 49 | 70 |
| Halifax | 12,687 | 7,620 | 4,916 | 2,933 | 1,230 | 557 | 4,486 | 3,893 | 1,996 | 237 | 59 | 0 |
| Harnett | 5,735 | 1,254 | 2,794 | 182 | 1,449 | 454 | 1,241 | 618 | 140 | 0 | 111 | 0 |
| Haywood | 1,100 | 4,032 | 213 | 1,906 | 0 | 212 | 887 | 1,914 | 0 | 0 | 0 | 0 |
| Henderson | 1,219 | 1,539 | 1,219 | 1,447 | 0 | 92 | 0 | 0 | 0 | 0 | 0 | 0 |
| Hertford | 6,113 | 3,383 | 2,691 | 973 | 60 | 284 | 2,981 | 2,113 | 332 | 13 | 49 | 0 |
| Hoke | 3,217 | 1,102 | 1,748 | 324 | 0 | 407 | 1,469 | 371 | 0 | 0 | 0 | 0 |
| Hyde | 3,363 | 887 | 1,084 | 321 | 0 | 0 | 2,279 | 566 | 0 | 0 | 0 | 0 |
| Iredell | 1,665 | 2,277 | 1,060 | 1,498 | 0 | 0 | 43 | 676 | 560 | 103 | 2 | 0 |
| Jackson | 121 | 1,491 | 121 | 1,208 | 0 | 283 | 0 | 0 | 0 | 0 | 0 | 0 |
| Johnston | 2,486 | 2,360 | 1,773 | 188 | 0 | 408 | 713 | 1,764 | 0 | 0 | 0 | 0 |

*continued*

**Table A.15—Roundwood timber product output by county, product, and species group, North Carolina, 2007 (continued)**

| County | All products Soft-wood | All products Hard-wood | Saw logs Soft-wood | Saw logs Hard-wood | Veneer logs Soft-wood | Veneer logs Hard-wood | Pulpwood[a] Soft-wood | Pulpwood[a] Hard-wood | Composite panels Soft-wood | Composite panels Hard-wood | Other industrial Soft-wood | Other industrial Hard-wood |
|---|---|---|---|---|---|---|---|---|---|---|---|---|
| | | | | | *thousand cubic feet* | | | | | | | |
| Jones | 13,116 | 1,758 | 5,553 | 0 | 1,449 | 3 | 6,114 | 1,755 | 0 | 0 | 0 | 0 |
| Lee | 2,915 | 1,055 | 1,961 | 906 | 724 | 4 | 97 | 145 | 0 | 0 | 133 | 0 |
| Lenoir | 4,702 | 1,328 | 1,932 | 0 | 543 | 5 | 2,227 | 1,323 | 0 | 0 | 0 | 0 |
| Lincoln | 2,375 | 1,707 | 2,076 | 1,320 | 0 | 0 | 159 | 387 | 140 | 0 | 0 | 0 |
| Macon | 882 | 2,698 | 283 | 970 | 0 | 8 | 599 | 1,720 | 0 | 0 | 0 | 0 |
| Madison | 397 | 2,322 | 397 | 1,684 | 0 | 638 | 0 | 0 | 0 | 0 | 0 | 0 |
| Martin | 10,990 | 2,053 | 7,165 | 889 | 0 | 69 | 3,825 | 1,095 | 0 | 0 | 0 | 0 |
| McDowell | 2,355 | 3,273 | 1,375 | 2,000 | 0 | 70 | 980 | 1,203 | 0 | 0 | 0 | 0 |
| Mecklenburg | 1,320 | 1,579 | 829 | 711 | 0 | 0 | 211 | 817 | 280 | 51 | 0 | 0 |
| Mitchell | 339 | 1,455 | 339 | 1,243 | 0 | 212 | 0 | 0 | 0 | 0 | 0 | 0 |
| Montgomery | 5,677 | 8,021 | 4,000 | 2,931 | 0 | 36 | 1,397 | 5,054 | 280 | 0 | 0 | 0 |
| Moore | 10,351 | 4,068 | 7,814 | 2,687 | 0 | 407 | 2,117 | 974 | 420 | 0 | 0 | 0 |
| Nash | 2,780 | 3,403 | 1,421 | 1,685 | 0 | 183 | 777 | 1,450 | 582 | 85 | 0 | 0 |
| New Hanover | 847 | 75 | 352 | 0 | 283 | 25 | 212 | 50 | 0 | 0 | 0 | 0 |
| Northampton | 9,322 | 5,885 | 2,272 | 1,474 | 70 | 305 | 6,349 | 4,093 | 582 | 13 | 49 | 0 |
| Onslow | 14,044 | 1,946 | 4,233 | 36 | 2,174 | 106 | 7,637 | 1,804 | 0 | 0 | 0 | 0 |
| Orange | 1,612 | 1,405 | 434 | 638 | 0 | 175 | 0 | 103 | 1,178 | 489 | 0 | 0 |
| Pamlico | 7,962 | 2,651 | 3,612 | 427 | 1,087 | 234 | 3,263 | 1,990 | 0 | 0 | 0 | 0 |
| Pasquotank | 1,706 | 1,657 | 972 | 255 | 0 | 0 | 715 | 1,402 | 0 | 0 | 19 | 0 |
| Pender | 9,557 | 1,390 | 4,212 | 525 | 708 | 250 | 4,597 | 615 | 0 | 0 | 40 | 0 |
| Perquimans | 2,847 | 519 | 2,024 | 19 | 0 | 0 | 804 | 500 | 0 | 0 | 19 | 0 |
| Person | 6,350 | 4,170 | 788 | 1,090 | 0 | 284 | 40 | 2,096 | 5,445 | 641 | 77 | 59 |
| Pitt | 10,076 | 4,673 | 5,172 | 429 | 724 | 723 | 4,180 | 3,521 | 0 | 0 | 0 | 0 |
| Polk | 2,361 | 1,611 | 1,057 | 900 | 0 | 0 | 1,024 | 711 | 280 | 0 | 0 | 0 |
| Randolph | 2,231 | 6,363 | 1,534 | 5,204 | 0 | 301 | 137 | 443 | 560 | 415 | 0 | 0 |
| Richmond | 7,502 | 1,354 | 5,724 | 820 | 0 | 407 | 1,778 | 127 | 0 | 0 | 0 | 0 |
| Robeson | 6,436 | 3,749 | 2,173 | 743 | 991 | 436 | 3,272 | 2,570 | 0 | 0 | 0 | 0 |
| Rockingham | 3,118 | 6,100 | 927 | 1,478 | 21 | 186 | 804 | 3,899 | 1,317 | 467 | 49 | 70 |
| Rowan | 2,380 | 4,294 | 1,385 | 1,311 | 0 | 43 | 155 | 2,837 | 840 | 103 | 0 | 0 |
| Rutherford | 3,147 | 8,422 | 1,635 | 2,020 | 0 | 70 | 1,326 | 6,332 | 140 | 0 | 46 | 0 |
| Sampson | 6,873 | 1,528 | 2,843 | 75 | 1,511 | 17 | 2,519 | 1,436 | 0 | 0 | 0 | 0 |
| Scotland | 3,344 | 1,198 | 1,016 | 300 | 849 | 413 | 1,479 | 485 | 0 | 0 | 0 | 0 |
| Stanly | 2,344 | 573 | 1,315 | 480 | 0 | 0 | 889 | 93 | 140 | 0 | 0 | 0 |
| Stokes | 2,535 | 4,161 | 1,240 | 2,884 | 0 | 0 | 118 | 636 | 1,121 | 571 | 56 | 70 |
| Surry | 1,923 | 3,278 | 1,004 | 2,224 | 0 | 0 | 37 | 535 | 841 | 519 | 41 | 0 |
| Swain | 90 | 662 | 90 | 662 | 0 | 0 | 0 | 0 | 0 | 0 | 0 | 0 |
| Transylvania | 24 | 207 | 24 | 207 | 0 | 0 | 0 | 0 | 0 | 0 | 0 | 0 |
| Tyrrell | 3,530 | 1,294 | 2,401 | 140 | 0 | 0 | 1,129 | 1,154 | 0 | 0 | 0 | 0 |
| Union | 2,520 | 3,464 | 709 | 329 | 867 | 0 | 664 | 3,084 | 280 | 51 | 0 | 0 |
| Vance | 2,582 | 1,865 | 892 | 652 | 881 | 228 | 190 | 985 | 565 | 0 | 54 | 0 |
| Wake | 7,263 | 4,768 | 4,189 | 353 | 724 | 211 | 2,073 | 4,204 | 188 | 0 | 89 | 0 |
| Warren | 7,883 | 6,304 | 3,085 | 2,126 | 1,065 | 365 | 2,423 | 3,417 | 1,081 | 66 | 229 | 330 |
| Washington | 5,957 | 1,311 | 3,993 | 381 | 0 | 132 | 1,964 | 798 | 0 | 0 | 0 | 0 |
| Watauga | 711 | 1,530 | 703 | 1,419 | 0 | 0 | 8 | 111 | 0 | 0 | 0 | 0 |
| Wayne | 6,215 | 2,193 | 2,606 | 0 | 2,174 | 52 | 1,103 | 2,128 | 332 | 13 | 0 | 0 |
| Wilkes | 2,357 | 6,201 | 2,161 | 3,594 | 0 | 1 | 193 | 2,399 | 0 | 207 | 3 | 0 |
| Wilson | 4,265 | 1,224 | 1,320 | 164 | 1,811 | 15 | 968 | 1,012 | 166 | 33 | 0 | 0 |
| Yadkin | 1,331 | 2,973 | 748 | 2,495 | 0 | 0 | 21 | 271 | 560 | 207 | 2 | 0 |
| Yancey | 372 | 3,065 | 372 | 2,782 | 0 | 283 | 0 | 0 | 0 | 0 | 0 | 0 |
| All counties | 473,704 | 254,680 | 244,657 | 103,760 | 35,911 | 14,505 | 151,350 | 129,059 | 39,403 | 6,356 | 2,383 | 1,000 |

[a] Includes roundwood delivered to nonpulpmills, then chipped and sold to pulpmills (4,608,000 cubic feet in 2007).

**Table A.16—Total roundwood output by product, species group, and source of material, North Carolina, 2007**

| Product and species group | All sources | Total | Growing-stock trees | | Other sources |
| | | | Sawtimber | Poletimber | |
| | | | *thousand cubic feet* | | |
| **Saw logs** | | | | | |
| Softwood | 244,657 | 240,868 | 234,619 | 6,249 | 3,789 |
| Hardwood | 103,760 | 102,662 | 96,022 | 6,640 | 1,098 |
| Total | 348,417 | 343,530 | 330,641 | 12,889 | 4,887 |
| **Veneer logs and bolts** | | | | | |
| Softwood | 35,911 | 35,226 | 34,166 | 1,060 | 685 |
| Hardwood | 14,505 | 14,343 | 14,343 | 0 | 162 |
| Total | 50,416 | 49,568 | 48,508 | 1,060 | 848 |
| **Pulpwood** | | | | | |
| Softwood | 151,350 | 145,643 | 54,056 | 91,587 | 5,707 |
| Hardwood | 129,059 | 126,530 | 40,816 | 85,713 | 2,529 |
| Total | 280,409 | 272,172 | 94,872 | 177,301 | 8,237 |
| **Composite panels** | | | | | |
| Softwood | 39,403 | 38,812 | 10,580 | 28,232 | 591 |
| Hardwood | 6,356 | 6,093 | 3,451 | 2,642 | 263 |
| Total | 45,759 | 44,905 | 14,031 | 30,874 | 854 |
| **Poles and posts** | | | | | |
| Softwood | 1,641 | 1,219 | 655 | 565 | 422 |
| Hardwood | 0 | 0 | 0 | 0 | 0 |
| Total | 1,641 | 1,219 | 655 | 565 | 422 |
| **Other miscellaneous** | | | | | |
| Softwood | 742 | 615 | 330 | 285 | 127 |
| Hardwood | 1,000 | 1,000 | 409 | 591 | 0 |
| Total | 1,742 | 1,615 | 739 | 876 | 127 |
| **Total industrial products** | | | | | |
| Softwood | 473,704 | 462,383 | 334,405 | 127,978 | 11,321 |
| Hardwood | 254,680 | 250,627 | 155,042 | 95,586 | 4,053 |
| Total | 728,384 | 713,010 | 489,446 | 223,564 | 15,374 |
| **Domestic fuelwood** | | | | | |
| Softwood | 8,892 | 7,877 | 4,580 | 3,297 | 1,015 |
| Hardwood | 46,183 | 39,939 | 29,214 | 10,725 | 6,244 |
| Total | 55,075 | 47,815 | 33,793 | 14,022 | 7,260 |
| **All products** | | | | | |
| Softwood | 482,596 | 470,260 | 338,984 | 131,275 | 12,336 |
| Hardwood | 300,863 | 290,566 | 184,255 | 106,311 | 10,297 |
| Total | 783,459 | 760,825 | 523,240 | 237,586 | 22,634 |

Numbers in rows and columns may not sum to totals due to rounding.

**Table A.17—Total roundwood output by species group, survey region, and ownership class, North Carolina, 2007**

| Species group and survey region | Total | Ownership class | | |
|---|---|---|---|---|
| | | Public | Forest industry | Nonindustrial private |
| | | *thousand cubic feet* | | |
| Softwoods | | | | |
| Southern Coastal Plain | 158,964 | 10,845 | 49,363 | 98,756 |
| Northern Coastal Plain | 178,858 | 249 | 40,948 | 137,661 |
| Piedmont | 124,364 | 482 | 9,387 | 114,495 |
| Mountain | 20,410 | 1,060 | 0 | 19,350 |
| Total softwoods | 482,596 | 12,636 | 99,698 | 370,262 |
| Hardwoods | | | | |
| Southern Coastal Plain | 46,439 | 364 | 2,176 | 43,898 |
| Northern Coastal Plain | 74,611 | 0 | 2,663 | 71,948 |
| Piedmont | 125,561 | 0 | 10,959 | 114,602 |
| Mountain | 54,252 | 2,236 | 0 | 52,016 |
| Total hardwoods | 300,863 | 2,601 | 15,798 | 282,464 |
| All species | 783,459 | 15,237 | 115,496 | 652,726 |

Numbers in rows and columns may not sum to totals due to rounding.

**Table A.18—Total roundwood output by species group, detailed species group, and product, North Carolina, 2007**

| Species group and detailed species group | Total | Saw logs | Veneer logs | Pulpwood | Composite panels | Poles and posts | Other miscellaneous | Domestic fuelwood |
|---|---|---|---|---|---|---|---|---|
| | | | | *thousand cubic feet* | | | | |
| Softwood | | | | | | | | |
| Cedar | 6,420 | 3,718 | 268 | 1,408 | 848 | 29 | 31 | 118 |
| Longleaf-slash pine | 15,498 | 9,532 | 955 | 4,570 | 121 | 34 | 0 | 286 |
| Eastern white pine | 7,575 | 4,747 | 0 | 1,619 | 1,069 | 0 | 0 | 139 |
| Loblolly-shortleaf pine | 383,024 | 192,274 | 31,649 | 127,111 | 22,966 | 1,396 | 569 | 7,060 |
| Other yellow pines | 62,783 | 29,685 | 3,031 | 14,341 | 14,265 | 162 | 143 | 1,157 |
| Cypress | 5,237 | 3,055 | 3 | 1,931 | 134 | 19 | 0 | 96 |
| Hemlock | 2,058 | 1,646 | 4 | 370 | 0 | 0 | 0 | 37 |
| Total softwoods | 482,596 | 244,657 | 35,911 | 151,350 | 39,403 | 1,641 | 742 | 8,892 |
| Hardwood | | | | | | | | |
| Soft maple | 29,942 | 9,915 | 1,506 | 13,079 | 780 | 0 | 65 | 4,597 |
| Hard maple | 1,214 | 869 | 48 | 90 | 20 | 0 | 0 | 186 |
| Hickory | 5,349 | 2,013 | 245 | 1,918 | 335 | 0 | 16 | 821 |
| Beech | 3,684 | 2,204 | 152 | 736 | 19 | 0 | 8 | 566 |
| Ash | 1,304 | 437 | 47 | 552 | 63 | 0 | 5 | 200 |
| Black walnut | 599 | 329 | 45 | 123 | 4 | 0 | 6 | 92 |
| Sweetgum | 61,016 | 16,435 | 4,067 | 30,101 | 942 | 0 | 105 | 9,366 |
| Yellow-poplar | 53,097 | 20,002 | 1,868 | 21,189 | 1,696 | 0 | 193 | 8,150 |
| Blackgum-tupelo | 11,873 | 3,095 | 933 | 5,927 | 93 | 0 | 2 | 1,823 |
| Sycamore | 1,925 | 529 | 72 | 1,006 | 23 | 0 | 0 | 296 |
| Black cherry | 2,167 | 824 | 99 | 788 | 120 | 0 | 3 | 332 |
| Select white oaks | 38,135 | 12,699 | 1,083 | 17,807 | 576 | 0 | 116 | 5,853 |
| Other white oaks | 16,196 | 7,231 | 849 | 5,377 | 220 | 0 | 33 | 2,486 |
| Select red oaks | 11,315 | 5,960 | 414 | 3,031 | 140 | 0 | 33 | 1,737 |
| Other red oaks | 46,163 | 15,161 | 2,370 | 20,156 | 1,042 | 0 | 348 | 7,087 |
| Elm | 3,524 | 1,193 | 137 | 1,602 | 44 | 0 | 7 | 541 |
| Other eastern hardwoods | 13,360 | 4,864 | 572 | 5,576 | 238 | 0 | 58 | 2,051 |
| Total hardwoods | 300,863 | 103,760 | 14,505 | 129,059 | 6,356 | 0 | 1,000 | 46,183 |
| All species | 783,459 | 348,417 | 50,416 | 280,409 | 45,759 | 1,641 | 1,742 | 55,075 |

Numbers in rows and columns may not sum to totals due to rounding.

**Table A.19—Total roundwood output by species group, detailed species group, and ownership class, North Carolina, 2007**

| Species group and detailed species group | Total | Ownership class | | |
|---|---|---|---|---|
| | | Public | Forest industry | Nonindustrial private |
| | | *thousand cubic feet* | | |
| Softwood | | | | |
| Cedar | 6,420 | 267 | 66 | 6,087 |
| Longleaf-slash pine | 15,498 | 92 | 6,627 | 8,779 |
| Eastern white pine | 7,575 | 24 | 0 | 7,551 |
| Loblolly-shortleaf pine | 383,024 | 9,071 | 87,616 | 286,337 |
| Other yellow pines | 62,783 | 2,995 | 5,246 | 54,543 |
| Cypress | 5,237 | 0 | 144 | 5,093 |
| Hemlock | 2,058 | 187 | 0 | 1,871 |
| Total softwoods | 482,596 | 12,636 | 99,698 | 370,262 |
| Hardwood | | | | |
| Soft maple | 29,942 | 228 | 1,417 | 28,297 |
| Hard maple | 1,214 | 0 | 0 | 1,214 |
| Hickory | 5,349 | 72 | 19 | 5,257 |
| Beech | 3,684 | 0 | 39 | 3,645 |
| Ash | 1,304 | 0 | 0 | 1,304 |
| Black walnut | 599 | 10 | 0 | 589 |
| Sweetgum | 61,016 | 6 | 1,912 | 59,098 |
| Yellow-poplar | 53,097 | 475 | 2,314 | 50,308 |
| Blackgum-tupelo | 11,873 | 17 | 478 | 11,378 |
| Sycamore | 1,925 | 0 | 266 | 1,659 |
| Black cherry | 2,167 | 67 | 121 | 1,979 |
| Select white oaks | 38,135 | 552 | 2,906 | 34,677 |
| Other white oaks | 16,196 | 53 | 815 | 15,328 |
| Select red oaks | 11,315 | 879 | 31 | 10,405 |
| Other red oaks | 46,163 | 135 | 5,342 | 40,686 |
| Elm | 3,524 | 0 | 4 | 3,520 |
| Other eastern hardwoods | 13,360 | 107 | 133 | 13,120 |
| Total hardwoods | 300,863 | 2,601 | 15,798 | 282,464 |
| All species | 783,459 | 15,237 | 115,496 | 652,726 |

Numbers in rows and columns may not sum to totals due to rounding.